DEDICATION

This book is dedicated to the love we share
with one another,

To friendships far and near,

And to my family, so precious and dear.

To cancer survivors praying and believing in God
for their healing

I love you, Mama!

FEAR THOU NOT; FOR I AM
WITH THEE, BE NOT DISMAYED;
FOR I AM THY GOD:
I WILL STRENGTHEN THEE.
YEA, I WILL HELP THEE;
YEA, I WILL UPHOLD THEE WITH THE
RIGHT HAND OF
MY RIGHTEOUSNESS.

———

ISAIAH 41:10 KJV

Fear Not,
ALL IS WELL

A Journey of Faith, Hope, and Survival

A MEMOIR

DR. SANDRA HENRY

Walton Publishing House

Houston, Texas

www.waltonpublishinghouse.com

Printed in the United States of America

The advice found within may not be suitable for every individual. This work is purchased with the understanding that neither the author nor the publisher is held responsible for any results. Neither author nor publisher assumes responsibility for errors, omissions, or contrary interpretations of the subject matter herein. Any perceived disparagement of an individual or organization is a misinterpretation.

All scriptures are taken from The Holy Bible: KJV, ESV NKJV, NIV, TPT

Please take note that Walton Publishing style and the author capitalizes certain pronouns in Scripture that refer to the Father, Son, Holy Spirit, and may differ from some publisher's styles.

Brand and product names mentioned are trademarks that belong solely to their respective owners.

Library of Congress Cataloging-in-Publication Data under

ISBN: 978-1-953993-52-6 (Paperback)

ISBN: 978-1-953993-49-6 (Digital/ E-book)

> **BEHOLD, HOW GOOD AND PLEASANT IT IS FOR BRETHREN TO DWELL TOGETHER IN UNITY.**
>
> ———
>
> **PSALM 133.1 NKJV**

CONTENTS

⸽ ⸽

FOR WITH GOD NOTHING WILL BE IMPOSSIBLE.

———

LUKE 1:37 NKJV

INTRODUCTION

> *"You shall love the Lord your God with all your heart, with all your soul, and with all your mind. This is the first and greatest command. And the second is like it; You shall love your neighbor as yourself."*
>
> ~ MATTHEW 22:37-39 NKJV

> *"And Jabez called on the God of Israel saying, "Oh, that You would bless me indeed, and enlarge my territory, that Your Hand would be with me, and that You would keep me from evil, that I may not cause pain!" So, God granted what him what he requested."*
>
> ~I CHRONICLES 4:9-10 NKJV

This book was inspired by God and written to all of you with blessings of hope. It does not tell the entire story of my life, but I pray it will demonstrate the Power of God, His love, and His mercy in my life. He encouraged me to step out of my comfort zone and to do His Will. I pray what has been revealed to you will allow you to witness His glory and believe in Him. I remain humble in His presence and obedient to His Word that has sustained me all these years. I can truly testify to His love, and I know Him to be true. I can also testify to His protection for those He calls His own. He continues to share His sovereign will over my life purpose and destiny. Yet, He gives us all freedom to come to Him and love Him without restraints or demands.

In my life, I can truly express to everyone, God has kept every promise He made to me. During my experience with cancer, He whispered to me "Fear Not All Is Well, I Am with Thee." I believed Him from the moment I heard those words spoken to me and I cling to them today. I am still in awe with the greatness of God. I pray my life will inspire and motivate someone to not give up, but to keep going in the face of adversity and more than anything else, put God first.

Losing my mother at an early age was devastating, but finding a loving God was a tremendous blessing and a precious life changing experience. He was always right there waiting for me. He continued to preserve and protect me even when I rejected Him. He continued to wait for the door to my heart to open and for me to ask for forgiveness. I am so thankful I invited Him in wholeheartedly. It is the best decision I have ever made in my life.

As you read this book, I pray that you will reverence His awesomeness and depend on Him when you are glad and when you are sad, as I do. I pray your relationship with our Father will be magnified and your love for Him will become intimate. I am so grateful for the opportunity to serve Him and go where He commands me. He loves us unconditionally and He wants you and me to live a prosperous life in every way. He is our Father and our refuge in a troubled world.

I pray you will walk away with a renewed strength and not allow fear to hinder your destiny. Knowing you are valuable and there is no limit to what you can accomplish on your life journey through Jesus Christ. Keep the Faith! Pray and believe God for all things!

Grace be with you,

THE SPIRIT OF THE LORD HAS MADE ME, AND THE BREATH OF THE ALMIGHTY GIVES ME LIFE.

JOB 33:4 ESV

CHAPTER 1:

IN THE BEGINNING: IT HAPPENED TO ME!

————— ᴕᴕᴕ —————

MY BATTLE WITH CANCER

May 21, 2015, was a beautiful day full of hope for the future and I was finally on my way to Baylor Scott and White Hillcrest Medical Center for an annual mammogram. With every breath I took and every move I made, my heart and soul whispered to me my Lord was with me, and I could feel His presence in my life. I had always been adamant about making sure I scheduled my yearly physical and mammogram on time. The courageous and compelling stories shared with me over the years, by cancer survivors, educated me on the importance of this health issue. They encouraged me to become proactive as a woman. Breast cancer is the type of cancer that forms in the cells of the breast. For women in the United States, breast cancer rates higher than any other cancer, besides lung cancer. Though not as common, men can develop breast cancer too (1 in 833).

As an advocate for breast cancer survivors since 1990, I am passionate about being an active participant in fighting for a cure in our communities. [1]Statistically about one in eight women will develop invasive breast cancer over the course of her lifetime. For women in the United States, breast cancer rates are higher than any other cancer, except for lung cancer. To my knowledge, no one in my immediate family had ever been diagnosed with breast cancer. Becoming an advocate and starting a foundation dedicated to survivors, was something God compelled me to do. I believe God called me for this journey and life's purpose because their lives and voices matter.

[1] Baylor Scott and White Health 2021, bswhealth.com

It was my standard practice to have my annual mammogram around my birthday in January. That was how I remembered to make my appointment and keep on schedule. In 2015, things were different, and my circumstances changed. My primary doctor moved and was no longer available, forcing me to find another doctor. It took some time and the grace of God to find a good one. Many doctors do not readily take on new patients, even with excellent health insurance. I prayed to God, "Lord, this is so important. I really need You! Please help me find a doctor. I know You are with me, and I trust You! Please show me what to do. I am desperate!" I truly needed His guidance.

One day, Angie, our daughter, stopped by our house, and I shared my circumstances with her. She offered me the name and number of her primary doctor and suggested I give her a call. I called the doctor that same day. Praise God she had an opening! My prayers were answered! I will always be grateful to Angie for her help and understanding that day. When God opens a door for you, run, do not walk through it. Go without hesitation or doubt. Trust and believe in Him.

> *"Trust in the Lord with all your heart, and do not lean on your own understanding. In all your ways acknowledge Him, and He will make straight your paths."*
>
> (PROVERBS 3:5-6 ESV)

A Day of Hope

> *"The Lord delights in those who fear Him, who put their faith in His unfailing love."*
>
> ~PSALM 147:11 NIV

So that special day in May 2015, I was excited and anxious to get my mammogram procedure done. Can you believe it! I was actually glad to see a doctor and have a medical procedure done. Wow! It was not the procedure but the possibility of a positive outcome that caused my excitement. I wanted to live and spend time with my family.

That morning I dressed in my favorite blue denim dress with a short white mesh jacket and beige sandals. I just wanted to look and feel special that day. Have you ever felt that way after a complex situation? I arrived early with confidence in Christ that everything would be okay. I was not worried at all about it. God had answered my prayers, and that was all that mattered. He gave me the gift of hope without fear.

The office and its admittance procedure were familiar to me. I walked up to the check-in window and spoke to the receptionist, who requested that I sign in and take a seat in the waiting area. The office staff was always so friendly, and this was no different. The television played in the background; however, I do not remember what was on. I was just so focused on completing the insurance and medical history paperwork. The atmosphere and décor evoked a calming, relaxing, and stress-free ambiance. There was also coffee and tea available, but I chose not to indulge myself in either of them. I completed the paperwork and waited for my name to be called. Mission Accomplished!

My mind began to wander to my family, and I started to think about our youngest son's, Devlin, upcoming birthday. We always had a special time for family birthdays. My daydream was interrupted by the call of my name by the nurse. I jumped up and followed her down the hall to prepare for the procedure. I entered the changing room and changed my clothes. I wiped the deodorant from my underarms and around the area for the imaging as instructed by the nurse. First, I had to put the weird hospital gown on! I am sure many of you know exactly what I am talking about, in one word, YUK!

I locked my clothes in one of the nearby lockers and sat in another waiting area. My mind was still in a good place and free of worry. I spent the next few minutes thinking of Joseph, my husband, and what we would do later that day. I sat thinking of everyday thoughts as I waited for my routine procedure.

Finally, my name was called for the mammogram examination. I was asked some identifying questions, and afterward, the mammographer asked me to step onto the machine and place my breast in the proper place for the images—first the left and then the right breast. I had forgotten how cold the metal felt on my skin. She took images from different angles so the doctor could see every portion of the breasts. The procedure only took a few minutes, and the conversation was light. We talked about the coldness of the machine and the room. I thought, with scientific technology, it seemed to me by now we could figure out how to warm these machines." As women, that is the least of our concerns. We want to live! We want to be healthy, live with our families, enjoy our lives, and be treated with dignity. We want medical professionals to listen to us. We want to be heard and for them to focus on keeping us whole.

The mammogram procedure was conducted with the most advanced technology. I thank God for where He has allowed medicine to pioneer and grow. The gift of life comes from God. The scripture clearly says, "This is what the Lord, the God of your father, David says, I have heard the prayers and see your tears, I will heal you."

2 Kings 20:5 ESV;

> "For I am the Lord who hears you."
> ~EXODUS 15:26 ESV

The coldness of the machine is of little importance, but the compassion and mercy felt by every patient from their physician and medical staff have an enormous impact on their relationship, healing, and care. The mammographer escorted me back to the waiting area while the doctor reviewed the images. While I sat waiting for the results, I began to pray silently.

"

HEAR MY PRAYER, O 'LORD, AND LET MY CRY COME TO YOU. DO NOT HIDE YOUR FACE FROM ME IN THE DAY OF MY TROUBLE; INCLINE YOUR EAR TO ME; IN THE DAY THAT I CALL.

—

PSALM 102:1-2 ESV

CHAPTER 2:

AN UNUSUAL CIRCUMSTANCE

A little while later, something unusual happened. Instead of her saying to me I can go home as usual, she wanted me to follow her back into the imaging room. She stated the doctor wanted me to come back tomorrow for additional images. Since this had happened to me once before, I thought nothing of it. She stated the doctor wanted me to come back tomorrow for additional images. Since this had happened to me once before, I thought nothing of it.

The first time this happened to me, I was fearful, shocked, and worrisome. It was explained to me afterward that the shape of my breast and its structure caused them to pause and look deeper. According to the National Breast Cancer Foundation, Inc., "Mammograms can often show a breast lump before it can be felt. They also can show tiny clusters of calcium called micro-calcifications. Lumps or specks can be caused by cancer, fatty cells, or other conditions like cysts. Further tests are needed to find out if abnormal cells are present."

I am thankful they took the extra step in my care, and there was no cause for alarm then. However, this was considered a red flag, and they began to monitor me more closely. I returned the next day and repeated the same procedure as the day before. As I waited in the waiting room area, the mammographer escorted me back into the imaging room. This time, I was seated face to face with the doctor who reviewed my images. She was so compassionate and caring as she spoke those horrifying words that I never wanted to hear echoing in my ears and mind.

"The results of the mammogram discovered a small mass on your right breast, and we need to schedule you for a biopsy immediately to determine what kind of treatment is necessary," she said. At that moment, my entire world was shaken! The room seemed to close in, and I felt so alone. That was not the news I had expected to hear. I needed my family there, but I had not asked anyone to come with me. After all, it was just a routine visit! There was no reason for me to think differently. I did not feel sick. I had not detected any problems through self-examination.

According to the American Cancer Society, "when breast cancer is detected early, and is in the localized stage, the 5-year relative survival rate is 99%. Early detection includes doing monthly breast self-exams, scheduling regular clinical breast exams, and mammograms". I cannot stress enough the importance of self-examinations, mammograms, and prayer.

At this point, things were moving rather swiftly. I was about to undergo one of the most painful medical experiences in my life next to childbirth. I had never had a biopsy done before and had no idea what to expect. The medical staff explained the procedure, but some things must be experienced, and not every emotional feeling can be explained. This is where faith in God steps in. All I had been taught and believed was about to be on the line. The biopsy was to determine if the mass was cancerous. And if so, what was the best course of action to take in defeating it. What were my options? Grab hold of life and do not let go, I thought to myself.

As I lay on the operating table face down with my breast fitted in that hole, I could hear the idle chatter of the medical staff. I prayed that God would help me through this unbearably painful ordeal. I prayed the agony of the biopsy would be over quickly. I prayed the result would not reveal cancer, and if so, my doctor would be able to treat or remove it. Yes, I was afraid of the outcome. Yet, in my spirit, I felt the presence of God.

His Spirit transformed me into an unexplainable calmness. The nurse reassured me they were almost done, but I did not answer. I continued to meditate with my Father and received His peace. We had been through so much in my life, and I knew He was with me now. Even though thoughts of death did linger in my mind, I felt His security in my heart. I had to surrender all my anxieties and emotions to Him and surrender to His will. I needed my Father, and He was right there for me. When the biopsy was finally over, I had to seek God for His sustaining power and His wisdom. I had to wait! I had to be patient and wait on God. For many of us, waiting is not so easy to do. But like in any situation, God is still in control. His sovereign will be done.

As we wait on the Lord to determine the outcome in any situation, waiting is a process and a rebirthing experience. We may wonder, "Did God hear my prayer?" and "How long must I wait?" If we are not careful, doubt will begin to enter our spirit when our faith is tested. In the wait, we can begin to get tired and weary. Our hope can fade, and strength can weaken, allowing us to slip into darkness easily. In those moments, we must change our focus and remind ourselves to "delight ourselves in the Lord and He will give us the desires of our hearts."

Simply draw closer to Him and find peace in the tranquility of His love. In the wait, I am comforted by helping others, I love working in the garden to relieve stress, and reading the Bible is soothing to my spirit and gives me hope. I can call a dear friend and share my thoughts for encouragement and prayer. Listening to my favorite genre of my music calms my spirit in the wait. I encourage you to do those things that calm you in the wait and keep you strengthened. We must stand firm and not become fearful because fear will weaken us and cause us to lose hope. Life does not come from what we have or what we do. Life comes from delighting ourselves in God, Himself. In the wait, we acknowledge God as our "True Source." It is up to His grace and mercy what will be the outcome. We praise and worship Him. We trust the One who is calling us to wait.

> *"Trust in the Lord with all your heart, and do not lean on your own understanding. In all your ways acknowledge Him, and He will make straight your path."*

I trust You, Lord!

BE STRONG AND
COURAGEOUS. DO NOT BE
AFRAID OR TERRIFIED
BECAUSE OF THEM, FOR THE
LORD YOUR GOD GOES WITH
YOU; HE WILL NEVER LEAVE
YOU NOR FORSAKE YOU.

DEUTERONOMY 31:6 NIV

CHAPTER 3:

MY DIAGNOSIS THE DOCTOR SAID...

⟿ ⟳ ⟲

The doctor informed me that the biopsy determined the mass had to be surgically removed. I was diagnosed with Carcinoma Type II Breast Cancer. As she was speaking, my first reactive thought was death! At that moment, I did not have any hope for my future. I was afraid and felt alone. My mind started to race with lots of questions. *Will I leave my husband and my family behind? Will I miss my grandchildren growing up, raising their families, and living life? Will my dreams end here in this way?*

I had more goals and aspirations I wanted to accomplish in my life, and I still felt capable of achieving them. I could not help but reflect on my mother's fight for her life as she lay on her dying bed riddled with illness and pain. *Will that be my fate also? How will I tell my family? God knows His children, and He knows how much we can bear.* I believe the church folks when they say, "He will not put more on us than we can bear." "Blessed is the man who remains steadfast under trial, for when he has stood the test he will receive the crown of life, which God has promised to those who love Him." (James 1:12 ESV)

Furthermore, God has a plan for all of our lives, and His timing is perfect. Even if we can bear more pain and suffering, His plan will be manifested at the perfect time, and He will embrace us with His love. The adversity we experience strengthens us for the Kingdom's work. God does not allow the testing to weaken us, and He always gives us a way to endure the pain. Jesus already paid the ultimate and most harsh price of pain and suffering with His life when He died on the cross for us. Yet, if we follow Him, we will have to endure some trials and tribulations in our life's journey. The question is, how will we bear our pain and suffering?

> *"No temptation (testing) has overtaken you*
> *except what is common to mankind. And God is*
> *faithful; He will not let you be tempted (tested)*
> *beyond what you can bear. But when you are*
> *tempted, He will also provide a way out so that*
> *you can endure it. "*
>
> ~1 CORINTHIANS 10:13 NIV

God instantly whispered in my ear, "Fear not, all is well." From that moment, my feelings of loneliness disappeared, and I believed the whispers of God and His promise to me. My faith was strengthened and renewed in my heart, mind, and spirit as I heard God speak to me. God's words immediately filled me with hope. I held onto my faith that I would make it through that ordeal. I knew my God was faithful and trustworthy. I knew His character, and I knew He always keeps His promises. God told me, "I got this," and I believed Him!

Life happens!

After all the circumstances I had been through in my life. After all the storms we had traveled through together, how could I do anything else but trust Him. You have to know God to know you can trust Him with everything. How do we trust God in all circumstances? How do we let go and let God? The story of Jesus resurrecting Lazarus from death reassures us that Jesus Christ is who He proclaimed to be the Son of God and the Messiah. Jesus was given power over death's stench and hideousness, and the resurrection breathes life. He has power over the Universe. I believe God!

The Bible said that Lazarus, Jesus' beloved friend, became gravely ill. Mary and Martha called for Jesus to come to pray and heal Him. "Lord, the one You love is sick." Jesus loved Mary, Martha, and Lazarus. He was in another city and away from Bethany. "When He heard this, Jesus said, "This sickness will not end in death. No, it is for God's glory so that God's Son may be glorified through it." (John 11:4 NIV) Jesus' delay in our circumstances is for a purpose and to glorify the Father. Sometimes Jesus will delay the outcome of our turmoil for a greater purpose. He still loves us, and He is still close. Trust Him in the process even when we do not see what He is doing.

> *"Then He said to the disciples, "Let us go back to Judea."*

~JOHN 11:7 NIV

Because of Jesus' safety, the disciples are reluctant. First, Jesus said, "Our friend Lazarus has fallen asleep; but I am going to wake him up."

~JOHN 11:11 NIV

Later, He spoke plainly and said, "Lazarus is dead."

~JOHN 11:14 NIV

Jesus waited. When He finally arrived, Lazarus had been in the tomb for four days, and Mary and Martha were in mourning for their brother. They were among the wailing women and the Jews. When Martha heard of Jesus' coming, she ran to meet Him. While Mary waited, Martha said to Jesus, "Lord, if you had been here my brother would not have died." "But I know that even now God will give You whatever You ask." (John 11:21-22 NIV)

I can only imagine the emotions and grief of Martha. She and her siblings walked with Jesus and knew of His miraculous power. She may have thought, why did You not come when I called You, Lord? How could You allow my brother, who You love, to suffer and die? Lord, where were You when I needed You? Does any of this sound familiar to you in your life or circumstances?

"Jesus said to her, "Your brother will rise again." (John 11:23 NIV) "Martha answered, "I know he will rise again in the resurrection at the last day." After they continued to speak, Jesus said to Martha, "I am the resurrection and the life. He who believes in Me will live, even though he dies and whoever lives and believes in Me will never die. Do you believe this?"

> *"Yes, Lord, she told Him, I believe that You are the Christ, the Son of God, Who was to come into the world."*
> **~JOHN 11:24-27 NIV**

When Mary heard Jesus had come, she quickly ran to meet Him, and the mourners followed her. When she reached Jesus, she fell at His feet and wept. She said to

Jesus, "Lord, if You had been here, my brother would not have died." The scripture said, "When Jesus saw her weeping, and the Jews who had come along with her also weeping, he was deeply moved in spirit and troubled. Jesus Wept." (John 11:29-35 NIV) All the mourners there were witnesses of His compassion and great love.

Jesus asked, "Where have you laid him?" Jesus once again deeply moved, asked, "Take away the stone." Martha cried out that there would be a stench because he had been in the grave for four days. Then Jesus reminded Mary, "Did I not tell you that if you believe, you would see the glory of God?" Jesus knew Lazarus would rise from death but wept because He is compassionate and filled with love for us. Jesus' life, death, and resurrection are most important in the life of a believer. It is where our faith is built. The resurrection is the triumph and glorious victory for every believer. It validates everything Jesus said can be trusted and is the fulfillment of the scriptures and God's Word.

So, they took away the stone. Jesus looked to heaven and said, "Father, I thank You that You have heard Me, but I said this for the benefit of the people standing here, that they may believe that You sent me. Jesus called in a loud voice, "Lazarus, come out!" (John 11:36-44 NIV)

Lazarus came forward! From that moment, some people believed and put their faith in Him, Jesus Christ.

In this story, we are reminded of two extraordinary truths. The first one is that Jesus Christ took the weight and punishment of this entire world with compassion and love. He died so we would have a relationship with the Father. The second truth is that Jesus revealed His power over death to the world while glorifying our Father in heaven. As a result, those who believe in Him will receive spiritual life. We can trust Him with every circumstance because of His love for us and His power to change any situation.

No, I was not alone, and because of my relationship with Jesus, I knew He would see me through. God was not only going to walk with me, but He would also see to the needs of my family and those who loved me. I could go home with a heart filled with His peace. He will do the same for you if you seek Him, build your relationship with Him, and believe in His promises. When our situation seems bleak and discord is everywhere, we can have faith in the Son of God and worship a Father, who has given everything for His children.

> *"To everything there is a season, and a time to every purpose under the heaven"*
>
> ~ECCLESIASTES 3:1KJV

I believe God!

God's Gift of Life

> *"For I, the Lord Your God, hold your right hand; it is I who say to you, "Fear not, I am the One Who helps you."*
>
> ISAIAH 41:13 ESV

When I finally arrived home, I shared my experience of the day, my ordeal, and the doctor's diagnosis with my husband, Joseph. He is my love, my friend, and my quiet strength. I felt what Joseph's reaction would be before he spoke. His mind would be saying, "How can I fix this?" But his heart would be asking, "God, please help us through this. We need You." We are a praying family and believers in the way of Jesus Christ.

The next person I shared my experience with was Devlin. He has a soothing strength that makes it easy to talk to him and a comforting spirit that allows people to confide in him. God blessed him with the spirit of a compassionate heart for others as a young boy. Devlin and I have maintained a bond from the day he was born. In many ways, we are alike. As I shared the news with him, he was speechless, but his heart and his body language spoke volumes. "Lord, I can't lose my Mom. Please, God, help us."

How do I really know all of this? Some years later, I asked Joseph and Devlin how they felt when I shared the news about my breast cancer diagnosis, and they shared these words with me. After 36 years of marriage, we sometimes feel what the other is feeling without uttering a word; sometimes, we can finish each other's sentences, especially in an emotionally intense situation like that was.

The next person was our daughter, Angie (Angela), and I thank God for filling her heart with compassion to walk with me in my time of need. As you may recall, Angie recommended my primary doctor to me.

I also shared this distressful news with my biological sister, Diane (who was later diagnosed with breast cancer in 2016), Aunt Catherine (my dear Uncle Henry's widow), Shawann and Tyshema (my two nieces and Diane's daughters). Their first reaction was shock, and then the questions of what to do followed. Shawann was a registered nurse at Duke University until she decided to work as a traveling nurse. Sadly, she passed away in March 2020 during the Corona Virus Pandemic. God's glory reigns in each of us who love Him and are chosen by Him.

I shared the news with my dear friend and breast cancer survivor, Janice Matthews. Janice prayed with me, promised to walk with me, and be near my side throughout that traumatic experience. Janice is still with me in friendship and love until this very day, and I am with her in the same way.

My sisters in Christ, Rev. Dr. Mary Lynn Hamilton and Pat James, rushed to my home with prayers on their lips and in their hearts for me. We have had to fight so many spiritual and emotional battles together. Pat James would later battle cancer herself. Yet, we remain prayer warriors for Christ and dear friends.

Later, I shared the news with my dearest friends, sisters in the ministry, others in the family, and prayer warriors. I would grow to need all of them more in the days that were ahead. God surrounded me with love, and I continued to remember His words to me, "Fear not, all is well." No, I was not alone! It did not take long for those who genuinely love me to surround and shower me with love in many ways.

My church, Abundant Love Fellowship Church in Hewitt, Texas, Pastor Edward L. Ross and Sis. Shelia Ross surrounded my family and me with chains of prayers and gifts of love. My dear friends texted me with words of encouragement and called me with uplifting words of hope. Everyone was anxious to help in any way. All I had to do was ask. Never for another moment did God allow me to feel or think about being alone. God placed some incredibly special and amazing people in my life, and we remain together today. Thank You, Lord, for blessing me with angels on earth.

> *"There is no fear in love, but perfect love casts out fear. For fear has to do with punishment, and whoever fears has not been perfected in love."*
>
> (1 JOHN 4:18 ESV)

God's Perfect Love!

"

I THANK MY GOD UPON EVERY REMEMBRANCE OF YOU...

PHILIPPIANS 1:3 NKJV

CHAPTER 4:

UNVEILING MY LIFE JOURNEY

―――――――ↄↄↄↄ―――――――

MY MAMA

> "In the morning I Rise"
>
> "It's difficult but far from impossible and we smile more than we cry."
>
> ~ACTRESS REGINA KING

cannot express how I managed to cope with my cancer experience or life journey without unveiling a glimpse into my past and the endurance of its challenges. My strength is rooted in my God, my family, and my Mama. I could not come through any traumatic experience without my God's help. I rely on the treasures of life my Mama left me and the love of God with His Wisdom to see me through hardening situations. I can smile a joyful smile of contentment.

I was raised by a single mother, Henrietta Williams, from Gadsden, Alabama. She worked hard and died too early. I vaguely remember my father because he left us a long time ago. I lived in New York City, New York, with my family from childhood until adulthood. In the "Big Apple," as it is famously called, life was not always easy for my Mama, but faith, grit, love for her children, and perseverance motivated her not to give up. There were times in our childhood when we had no Christmas toys in our home. *Have you ever experienced that as a kid? Can you imagine as a child not having toys at Christmas?*

I can only wonder how my Mama felt. Sometimes we had to rely on government assistance (welfare department) to survive. Where we lived was not the best neighborhood, but we had a roof over our heads. At other times, we had what seemed like an abundance, but we always had love. One thing I constantly remember was the delicious smell of something good to eat cooking in the kitchen. We were never hungry and always had a home.

Reflecting on my childhood, I did not view us as being poor. I never thought of my life as living in poverty, although we did. Mama was determined to create a better life for her children. Some of you reading this may have had a similar upbringing as mine. Does my Mama remind you of your parents? Despite what many would consider a setback, she managed to move us into a modest lifestyle in the Bronx, New York. She had faith and perseverance. This faith walk is amazing. Prayer really does move mountains, hurdles, and hills. Our lives can change in the twinkling of an eye.

After we moved, we would soon have another mountain to climb. My mother became ill in my early teens, and I became her caregiver. She was diagnosed with kidney disease, which developed into acute renal failure. Or at least, that is what I was told. I changed the bandages around her tubes and urine bags. I cleaned her wounds after five operations to save her life. I ensured she took her medication and accompanied her to her doctor's appointments. This all happened while still attending school and caring for my baby sister, Diane.

It was a time of survival, and I needed to grow up quickly and learn how to take care of the household. Although I never mastered the art of cooking, we managed. My Mama knew she was dying, and one day she tried to have a conversation with us about her "last and final wishes." We were so young. It was hard for us to understand. How do you tell your young kids you are dying? How do you make plans for their future without you? How do you make them understand you must leave them forever? Who will take care of them when you are gone? I know this could not have been easy for her.

While other teenagers had parties, attended prom, and made great future expectations, I could not. Taking care of my mother and keeping the household was more important than my dreams. There were life and death decisions that had to be made. My Mama shared her strength with us, even in her last days. Her frail body touched my heart with love and compassion. I wished there was more I could do to save her. In her last moments of life, we shared special times. During the night, when the house was quiet, she would teach me about life, and I would listen. We bonded deeply.

My Mama died from acute renal failure at forty-three years old. I was with her when she took her last breath in our home. It was a solemn day and definitely insufferable! It was a dreadful time for our family. My sister was so young! My Mama had suffered through that disease and continuously showed us how to trust in God to the end. My older brother Troy left our family after Mama died, and we have not seen him for many years. None of us knew why he had left the family, or at least my sister and I did not know. I really do miss him and love him still.

I am thankful for the strength God gave to my Mama, our family, and me. I am thankful for the humility and grace He gave me to care for my dying mother. I know God kept her even in her pain, and I will see her again. I love you, Mama!

If you still have your Mama in her later years, you are blessed. Hug your Mama or call her with sweet words of gratitude.

Life Lessons

My Mama taught me so many life lessons. She taught me to work hard for what I want or need in life. To stand up for what is right. She also taught me to set goals for myself and to strive to achieve them. She inspired me to follow my dreams. My Mama loved her children in a special way, through sacrifice and a longing to keep us safe. We had to face the harsh reality of life quite early. As children, we faced its cruelty, disadvantages, and sufferings, feeling the sting of inequality, ignorance, and injustices. We were black children growing up in a white world. Like many children who grew up in our time, we had the "talk" about the world's reality.

We grew up with a compassionate heart and a passion for serving our brethren. We learned to value life and cling to our precious moments with gratitude. Love is indeed an action word. Did I feel loved? Did I know what it was like to be safe or simply be a kid? If my Mama, Henrietta had anything to do with it, the answer is unequivocally yes! She taught me firsthand how to fight for my children and to love them to the very end.

Thank you, Mama, for always making me feel special. Thank you for a mother's true love and sacrifice.

Because of my Mama's example, I am who I am today. I see her likeness in so many areas of my life. Her legacy lives on through me. She nurtured me, and empowered all of her children to celebrate their uniqueness. She was compassionate and cared about the plight of others. She loved life and her family. As I help others to fulfill their purpose, I see that light shining through me. I even notice our similarities in my likes and hobbies. My Mama loved baseball, and her favorite team was the Brooklyn Dodgers! She and I loved to dance together. Those were some of my best moments with her. She humbly thanked God for everything; I can say I do too.

What is different? Lots! My Mama was tall and slim. While I am my own person, petite in size. In my youth and as a woman, I did not struggle with weight gain as I do now in my later years. I have maintained a youthful appearance for most of my life. I always looked younger than my age. So did my Mama, Grandma, and Great Grandmama, Lula Johnson. I guess it is in our DNA. I still had to grow and mature into womanhood. I had to learn what season of faith I was walking through and how God would strengthen my walk.

When I was a child, we did not attend church on a consistent basis, but I remember listening to my Mama's prayers to the Father. I remember hearing her humming and singing hymnals in the kitchen. She had a beautiful voice to me. She loved to sing *Amazing Grace, Take Me to The Water, and Swing Low Sweet Chariot.* Mahalia Jackson was one of her favorite artists. Although my Mama was raised in the church, she preferred to listen to church service on the radio. She later watched Oral Roberts, and Billy Graham preach the Gospel of Jesus Christ on television. There are so many unforgettable memories.

My Grandma

I always had a yearning to know more about God, and it was my grandmother, Louise Milner, who God chose to plant the seed and nugget deep within me about Him. My Grandma was petite in stature like I am but tall in her faith. She loved the Lord and loved sharing Him with anyone who would listen. She was loved by her church and family and highly respected by her neighbors and community. She also loved mission work. We would visit her church when we visited her and Grandpa in Alabama.

My Grandma came to stay with us toward the end of my Mama's illness. When Mama died, Grandma asked me where I wanted the funeral arrangements done? Did I want her to take our Mama home? I said, yes! Grandma took Mama home to Gadsden, Alabama, and she was buried near my Great Grandma behind my Mama's cousin Lula Mae Johnson's home in a small cemetery. There were many people (family and friends) at the funeral, and the cars stretched for what seemed like miles as we drove to the cemetery.

My Great Grandma and Great Grandpa had thirteen children, and all of them had children! Some of you with large families would know what I mean and the feelings of togetherness. Within our family, there was a strong bond of love. It was a beautiful homegoing celebration! Yes! Today I look back and see the financial burden that was placed on my Grandma Louise. She sacrificed for her family and never asked for anything in return. I have had the opportunity to visit Mama's grave since the funeral.

My Grandma has been gone for many years now. She died in Florida at the age of ninety-nine.

The Men in The Family

I come from a family of public service and military service people, domestic workers, excellent cooks, and bakers. Today they are called essential workers and culinary artists. My heritage and generations of strength taught us no matter what you do in life, do it with excellence. Every job is important, and we ought to have a sense of integrity while we work. We were taught to maintain impeccable work ethics with a grateful attitude. Both my Mama and Grandma were uneducated in traditional schooling. They did not graduate from high school but encouraged and sacrificed for us to receive high education achievements. They were determined that we would succeed in education and life. They were honorable teachers of life and examples of living life with love, compassion, faith, and humility.

My Grandma taught me to put God first and to pray for everything. My fond memory of my Grandma is visiting her in Gadsden in the summer and eating homemade churned ice cream. Watching her make it caused my mouth to water for the first taste. My love for gardening was birthed from working with Grandma in her beautiful garden of many colors and a variety of plants and vegetables. My memories of us planting flowers together linger in my heart today. She raised chickens, and I learned to care for them. I would listen to stories of our past ancestors from my Grandma. She loved quilting and left some beautiful quilts when she passed. My Grandpa died from a heart attack doing what he loved - fishing in his boat on the lake near home.

He was the only Grandpa I ever knew. He was a gentle and soft-spoken man. I love you, Grandma and Grandpa Homer! I miss our telephone conversations and the bits of wisdom I received. You inspired and empowered me to grasp life and work toward making a difference in the lives of others. I treasure those simple memories spent with you, and I think about you when the situations and burdens of life become overbearing. I can hear your voice and ask the question in my mind, "What would grandma and grandpa say to me about this?"

My Uncle Henry was a thirty-year retired U.S. postal worker and a U.S. Army veteran. He was my Mama's only sibling and lived in Queens, New York. It was quite a distance to travel, but when my Mama needed help, Uncle Henry was always there for us; he always had his sister's back and was supportive. He was a blessing in many ways during my Mama's illness and death. I could lean on Uncle Henry when things became so unbearable and overwhelming that I lost hope. My Uncle Henry would step in and love me through the pain in such a gentle way. No question about it, my Uncle Henry loved us. He raised my baby sister, Diane, after Mama died. My Uncle Henry sadly died of Alzheimer's in his late eighties several years ago.

Dealing With Mama's Death

The death of my Mama angered me, and I became rebellious. I used to constantly ask myself, "Who am I?" I had feelings of abandonment and mistrust shadowing my life. Some of the choices I made in the darkness of my life were poor. Fear of not having my Mama to talk with about significant and intimate issues or to lean on was overwhelming. I married too early, and so it ended in divorce after several years. More pain! I did not attend college as my Mama wanted until later in my life. It took years to work through the pain of losing my Mama, and it still hurts today. Still, God continued to be with me.

Looking back, God was preparing me for Himself and His work. He did not give up on me, even while I smoked weed and cigarettes, partied with the wrong people, and drank homemade alcoholic beverages like Sangria or a little brandy or rum and Coke. I thank God I was never an alcoholic or drug addict. *There but for the Grace of God!* Today I do not think about having a smoke or alcohol. God removed the urge from me. I quit smoking over forty years ago. He waited patiently for me and never judged me harshly as the world sometimes does to broken people.

God will never put (allow) more despair on us than we can bear. What a true statement! He knows our breaking point and knows exactly when to appear and cover us with His blanket of love. It is sometimes ironic or even seems unfair how a particular situation can change the outcome or course of a person's life. How we can come to a fork in the road of life, and one decision can create havoc or calmness. I believe following and obeying His righteousness is key to our relationship with the Heavenly Father. In my heart, I knew my Mama was suffering. My Father God ended her suffering and took her home with Him. Losing my Mama was devastating, but God allowed me to witness her strength and love for Him as she fought for life so that. I would know how to defeat my enemy, breast cancer, in my struggle later in my life. My faith would be tested in this battle, but my family roots and generations of faithful servants of God would give me hope. They fought the good fight and left a legacy of God first for us never to give up. My God is bigger than cancer or any affliction, and my faith remains in Him. Thank you, Mama, for sharing with me the endurance of overcoming pain and facing the unknown with confidence in our Heavenly Father.

> *Come to me, all who labor and are heavy laden, and I will give you rest. Take my yoke upon you, and learn from me, for I am gentle and lowly in heart, and you will find rest for your souls.*
>
> ~MATTHEW 11:28-29 ESV

"Let not your hearts be troubled. Believe in God; believe also in me. In my Father's house are many rooms. If it were not so, would I have told you that I go to prepare a place for you? And if I go and prepare a place for you, I will come again and will take you to myself, that where I am you may be also..."

~JOHN 14:3 ESV

Planting Seeds of Hope

"

THE LORD WILL FIGHT FOR YOU, YOU NEED ONLY TO BE STILL.

EXODUS 14:14 NKJV

CHAPTER 5:

A LIFE CHANGING DECISION

———— ༄ ༄ ༆ ————

Every person diagnosed with cancer must decide with their physician, family, and our Lord what treatment options are best for them. Cancer does not care about race, age, ethnic background, religion or Christian belief, or sex. Its only desire is to destroy whoever or whatever is in its way. For that reason, according to medicine, a person diagnosed with cancer has a limited time to make a life-changing decision. My faith continues to tell me God has the final word.

He created medicine and will determine what is best for each of us. Yet, we all experience our situation differently. I was blessed not to feel any continuous physical pain like some cancer patients experience. Yes, there was some pain, but it was not long and lingering. I believe my journey is to know what it is like to be diagnosed with cancer and be there for those who suffer greatly. My pain is the thought of death so close and right at my door. My pain is knowing I cannot do anything about it, but my heart knows I can rely on my God.

Our soul waits for the Lord; he is our help and shield. Psalm 33:20

On June 20, 2015, I had a scheduled appointment at Baylor Scott and White Hillcrest Medical Center in Waco, Texas, for surgery to remove the mass discovered in my right breast. I thank God it was discovered early and did not spread to other organs of my body. I chose to have a lumpectomy and not have my complete breast removed.

There were nights that I prayed with tears streaming down my face. I tossed and turned, asking God to help me make this most important decision. What shall I do?

What is the best course of action for me? It is not about losing my breast but fighting for my life. Will the doctor be able to remove all the cancer? What will the surgeon find in the operating room when he performs the surgery? What will I look like in the mirror? Will this thing called cancer ever return? Will I regret my decision? I spoke with God, and I had no regrets. I believe He kept and guided my decision.

Some people dismiss what I went through because I did not suffer in agony for years like my dear sister and brother cancer survivors. But I won't allow them to dismiss my journey. Every day I look in the mirror and see the scar in my right breast, and I know how close I came to not being able to comfort other survivors, or hold my children close, or love my husband, or live my life. I look in the mirror and I am grateful.

I spoke to a bilateral breast cancer survivor who someone said to her, "I am so sorry for you!" How can you know the pain you have just inflicted on someone who is fighting for life? She has no reason to be sorrowful, she is alive! With every cancer survivor, there is pain. It may be physical, mental, or even spiritual. It may be all three at the same time, but there is pain. God wipes our tears and soothes our spirit with His love and compassion. I thank God I am alive, and I can tell you my story.

On the day of my surgery, my room was filled with love. My dear friend, Janice Matthews, stayed with me until I was sedated and ready for surgery. Shelia Ross came to visit with me, and I was surprised to see her because I hardly knew her at the time. I will always remember and love her for that cherished moment of kindness. My Husband, Joe (Joseph) was right by my side, quietly praying for me and observing everything. Devlin took time away from work to see my face and touch my hand. Angie was there to make sure I was okay. My daughter-in-law, Devlin's wife, Jasmine, and Darren our youngest grandson, were there and stayed with Joe during the surgery. They made sure Grandpa ate.

While I was waiting to go into surgery, we were joyful, and I only had thoughts of a hopeful future. The atmosphere in the room was filled with peace. There was not a moment during this time that I was fearful as I was spiritually and emotionally ready for what was about to take place. I still believed what God had promised.

When I woke up after surgery, my doctor informed me the cancer had not spread, and they were able to remove it all. Furthermore, I did not have to endure chemotherapy or radiation. Hallelujah! Thank You, Jesus! God kept His promise to me! He whispered in my ear, I believed, and He took great care of His child. I do not take any of this miracle of life lightly. I believed what our Heavenly Father told me when I heard His voice speaking to me at a time when I needed Him the most.

Today, when I look into the mirror, what do I see? I smile because I know I am alive, and I live my life with the idea that every moment is precious. It is amazing how a tiny foreign spot found in your body or vicious mass can change your perspective on how we see life. I am a woman with a mission to show the world that God keeps protecting me, keeps His promises, and that I have a purpose.

> *"This is the day that the Lord has made; we will rejoice and be glad in it."*
> ~PSALM 118:24 NKJV

Rejoicing in the Lord!

REJOICE ALWAYS, PRAY WITHOUT CEASING, IN EVERYTHING GIVE THANKS; FOR THIS IS THE WILL OF GOD IN CHRIST JESUS FOR YOU.

I THESSALONIANS 5: 16-18 NKJV

CHAPTER 6:

GOD'S GRACE AND MERCY

CANCER FREE

Today I am a breast cancer survivor, or even better a thriver of life. But more than that, I am a child of God and a Kingdom citizen. It is the only appropriate title I want or need to be called. God loved me so much that when He heard me crying, He wiped my tears and soothed my spirit. My God stretched out His Healing hands and healed me. Only the Lord can do such a merciful thing for one who belongs to Him. As I continue to say, I can never repay the gift of life. I can only live my life according to His will and be grateful for His unconditional love. What an inspiring and wonderous journey!

I thank God for my continued life journey and constantly seek Him for purpose and His plan for my life. Because my Father kept His promise to me, I can humbly testify of His faithfulness to all who will listen. I trusted and believed God and my life is victorious! He can do the same for you if you submit to His will. You are victorious! I dare you to trust God with your most intimate thoughts and deeply troubling situations.

I encourage you to build a relationship with Him who has all the answers and has your best interest in mind. His word says, I know the plans I have for you, not to harm you but to prosper you. Of course, life will continue to through its curve balls, but I continue to believe and trust God to be there and to guide me in any circumstance, storm, or troubled situation. I can walk in the garden and see the beautiful array of flowers blooming and can smell the sweet aroma of life. I know He is there with me. I thank God, He allowed me to be here on this earth to receive that distraught call from a cancer survivor who needs Him; to pray with him or her; to share with them the beauty of life; to take a walk with them in the park and console them with His love and His word. I thank God for continuing to remind me that "a friend loves at all times" in laughter and in painful situations.

I thank God for His strength and giving me the strength to keep saying to Him, "Here I am, Lord, send me." I am grateful for the journey and the true meaning of life. "Thou shall not have no other gods before me." (Exodus 20:2-17). God loves us and protects us from harm and wants our focus to be on Him.

"My mission in life is not to merely survive, but to thrive, and to do so with some passion, some compassion, some humor, and some style." Maya Angelou, author, memoirist, poet, actress, and civil rights activist.

> "Seek Ye first the Kingdom of God and His righteousness..."
> ~MATTHEW 6:33 KJV

God First!

VICTORIOUS IN CHRIST

Inspired by God and written by
Rev. Dr. Sandra Henry

Cancer can sicken me or cause me to become distraught,

But cancer cannot own me or take away my intimate and humble thoughts,

My soul, my heart, and my spirit I give to thee, Lord, a faithful and loving God.

Cancer can cause tears, and fears, and many days of sorrow,

But unshakeable faith can move mountains and the Son can shine on my tomorrows,

I know the possibilities in my life are endless with my Lord and Savior, Jesus Christ,

He remains by my side in this fight, strong and mighty is He!

I am constantly in His sight.

I know He walks with me and sees me through my days of agony and distress

I can hear Him gently whisper to me "You are fearfully and wonderfully made,"

Don't fret or stress.

I press forward in Victory!

With a smile on my face, I can erase the condemned case and tell the world how much He loves me!

"I press toward the mark for the prize of the high calling of God in Jesus Christ."

With God, all things are possible, and I know nothing can stop me from my destiny,

Because I believe in Him.

Not even cancer, nor principalities, or evil powers!

I believe God and I walk by faith!

I AM VICTORIOUS IN CHRIST JESUS

This section is

dedicated to cancer

patients, cancer

survivors, and the loved

ones that support them.

SWEET FRIENDSHIPS REFRESH THE SOUL AND AWAKEN OUR HEARTS WITH JOY, FOR GOOD FRIENDS ARE LIKE ANOINTING OIL THAT YIELDS THE FRAGRANT INCENSE OF GOD'S PRESENCE.

PROVERBS 27:9 TPT

CHAPTER 7:

A MESSAGE TO CANCER SURVIVORS

———————— ꞁꙅꙅ ————————

What was your first reaction when you were told you had cancer? How did you find the strength to go through the treatment?

I consider my cancer a blessing. That may be strange to say to some people, but God has blessed me with the gift of life, and I can share His love with others. I know what it is like to hear the words of a cancer diagnosis for the first time. I also know of God's healing power and His love that sustains us through any traumatic experience. I share God's goodness with others and give them hope. I surround them with the kind of love I received from my family, friends, other cancer survivors, and my dear church family.

God renewed my spirit each day of recovery, and my faith calmed my fears, offering new life expectations. The love of Christ compelled me to fight passionately for the gift of life even today. I live to continue my life journey through grace, and you can too. It is nothing we have earned, but it is a gift given to us by God simply because He loves us and wants our relationship to continue to grow.. I have something to share with other cancer survivors, and it's the love of Christ and His Healing Power. My life was spared to be the support system for those who need a shoulder to cry on, an ear to listen, and a heart to care.

"

SUIT UP IN THE FULL ARMOR OF GOD. THE SWORD OF THE SPIRIT, SHIELD OF FAITH, BREASTPLATE OF RIGHTEOUSNESS, HELMET OF SALVATION, BELT OF TRUTH, BOOTS OF PEACE

EPHESIANS 6

"

CHAPTER 8:

OVERCOMING THE SPIRIT OF FEAR

———— ❧ ❧ ❧ ————

Prayer Changes Things

God's Gift – *Sharing the blessings of Life through Christ with others!*

> "Finally, be strong in the Lord and in his mighty power. Put on the full armor of God, so that you can take your stand against the devil's schemes. For our struggle is not against flesh and blood, but against the rulers, against the authorities, against

the powers of this dark world and against the spiritual forces of evil in the heavenly realms.

Therefore, put on the full armor of God, so that when the day of evil comes, you may be able to stand your ground, and after you have done everything, to stand. Stand firm then, with the belt of truth buckled around your waist, with the breastplate of righteousness in place, and with your feet fitted with the readiness that comes from the gospel of peace.

In addition to all this, take up the shield of faith, with which you can extinguish all the flaming arrows of the evil one. Take the helmet of salvation and the sword of the Spirit, which is the word of God. And pray in the Spirit on all occasions with all kinds of prayers and requests. With this in mind, be alert and always keep on praying for all the Lord's people."

~EPHESIANS 6:10-18 NIV

One of the main things that attack the mind of cancer patients is fear. Family members and friends can also feel fear as they face the uncertainty of knowing if their loved one will survive. Fear is an area that tried to grip me as well. So, in this chapter, I thought it would be good to discuss fear and provide you with the tools to overcome it.

What is FEAR?

The Miriam Webster Dictionary defines fear as:

An unpleasant, often strong emotion caused by anticipation or awareness of danger.

1. An instance of this emotion
2. A state marked by this emotion

Anxious concern: solicitude

Profound reverence and awe especially toward God

Reason for alarm: danger

To be afraid of: expect with alarm.

Nelson's New Illustrated Bible Dictionary: What is the Biblical definition of fear?

A feeling of reverence, awe, and respect, or an unpleasant emotion caused by a sense of danger. Fear may be directed toward God with reverence or humankind, and their harmful intentions.

According to Nelson's Biblical Dictionary, there are categories of fear:

<u>*Fear: A reverence or respect*</u>

The Bible teaches that children are to respect their parents:

> *"Every one of you shall revere his mother and his father, and you shall keep my Sabbaths; I am the Lord your God."*
>
> **~LEVITICUS 19:3 NLT**

The scripture also declares,

> *"the fear (reverence) of the Lord is the beginning of knowledge..."*
>
> **~PROVERBS 1:7 NIV**

and also

> *"the beginning of wisdom..."*
>
> **~PROVERBS 9:10 NIV**

_Harmful Fear: A harmful fear is a sense of terror or
dread._

Believers are instructed not to fear humans. Because they
cannot ultimately harm us (God can make our enemies
our footstool, Psalm 110:1; Psalm 23). We do not have to
fear people because God's power reigns over all of life.

Let us take for an example the story of David and the
Giant, Goliath in 1 Samuel 16 – 1 Kings 2 NKJV.

> _King Saul and the Israelite Army were fearful of
> this great, larger-than-life, between seven and
> over nine feet tall giant, Goliath, but a scrawny
> David walked in faith and believed God would
> fight this battle and win the victory. Goliath was
> a champion who fought for the Philistine Army.
> The giant Goliath was slain because of David's
> belief in the power of God. How do we fight our
> Goliath? David looked at the Giant Goliath from
> a different perspective. He looked at the battle
> from God's point of view, spiritually. If we look
> at our giant Goliaths (life issues and
> circumstances) from God's point of view, we will_

realize God will fight for us and there is no reason to fear. We have already won the victory. He will work miracles in our lives and defeat our enemies (even cancer). Why? Because He is God, and nothing is impossible for Him. Because of His deep love for us, He will come when we are faithful and call on Him.

"Do not be afraid of those who kill the body but cannot kill the soul."

~MATTHEW 10:28 NIV

"Do not be intimidated in any way by your enemies. This will be a sign to them that they are going to be destroyed, but that you are going to be saved, even by God Himself."

~PHILIPPIANS 1:28 NLT

Unbelievers: On the other hand, the unbelievers have every reason to be panic-stricken at the thoughts of God for he stands condemned before Him. "Whoever believes in Him is not condemned, but whoever does not believe stands condemned already because they have not believed in the Name of God's One and Only Son." (JOHN 3:18 KJV)

Noah Webster's American Dictionary of The English Language defines fear as:
"To feel a painful apprehension of some impending evil; to be afraid of; to consider or expect the approach of an enemy or of a storm. To feel anxiety on account of some unexpected evil."

Keys to Overcoming the Spirit of Fear

How do we overcome the spirit of fear in the face of our daily life challenges?

In our world today, we are faced with an abundance of misinformation, distrust, anger, and deceit. There are diseases like COVID -19, cancer, diabetes, and others. Then there is the wickedness of those with uncontrollable urges to harm others. Our world appears to be more fear-filled than peace-filled. Fear can be triggered by the unknown like walking into a dark room or looking over a high cliff or speaking in front of a large crowd for the first time. Fear can also be caused when we do not take the time to learn about one another caused by biases, racial injustice, or discord.

Reactions to fear can have physical effects like when our heart may beat faster, or we may feel dizzy, or a "pit" in our stomach, or begin to sweat, or we may have difficulty sleeping. All these feelings are true, but we must realize that on our life journey, when we are faced with the spirit of fear, we cannot allow it to control us to the point we are afraid to follow God, or stifle our creativity, or pursue our purpose, or work toward our destiny. We cannot allow fear to hinder our blessings.

Since before our birth, God has given each of us a calling on our lives to be manifested in His perfect time. His Sovereign power still reigns in our world, and He is in control. Even though we may not always understand the outcome or why things happen, we must have faith and trust in Him to heal our brokenness.

Paul writes to Timothy in 2 Timothy 1:7 (CSB) *"For God has not given us a spirit of fear, but one of power, love, and sound judgment."* The Word of God is our tool to fight fear and destroy the enemy. We cannot let fear intimidate us into becoming silent and isolated. Through faith and the power of God, we can stand up. Look at all the people in the Bible. Ruth and Naomi, David, Joseph, and the woman with the issue of blood, to name a few. Look at what Jesus had to face! They stood firm in the face of fear.

Observe those God has chosen in your life. Look at those God has chosen in our history. Perhaps it was Big Mama with her many self-sacrifices and a strong belief that God would make a way in any circumstances or challenges. She prayed in her closet or in her quiet room for a change in her circumstances. She prayed for a miracle.

Fear can cause us to become prisoners:

> *"Then the man and his wife heard the sound of God walking in the garden at the time of evening breeze, and they hid from the Lord God among the trees in the garden."*
> ~GENESIS 3:8 NIV

God created Adam and Eve for a relationship with Him, but disobedience, deceit, and sin broke that relationship. Man was in a beautiful garden enjoying a blissful and peaceful life with God, but that relationship was broken because of unhealthy choices and the experience of sin. They became prisoners of fear and were unable to fully experience the freedom of their relationship with God any longer.

When we become prisoners of fear, we want to hide from everyone, especially God. Our fears can keep us in bondage and isolation. It took the life, death, and resurrection of God's only Son, Jesus Christ, to form the bridge and build our relationship with God. Through prayer and worship, we can shift our eyes toward the One who changes our darkness into the light of liberation. We can conquer the spirit of fear through the love of Christ and His power-filled faith when faced with adversity or opposition. Go ahead, apply for that job you have been praying about but afraid to step out in faith. You have the victory. The older (seasoned) saints used to say, "When one door closes another one opens. Keep the faith! It is worth the work and the time.

WARNING:

Fear can restrict and hamper our FOCUS

Armed with Ammunition

> *"Commit your work to the Lord, and your plans will be established."*
>
> ~**PROVERBS 16:3 ESV**

> *"All Scriptures is breathed out by God and profitable for teaching, for reproofing, for correction, and for training in righteousness, that the man of God may be competent, equipped for every good work."*
>
> ~**2 TIMOTHY 3:16 ESV**

> *"Study and do your best to present yourself to God approved, a workman (tested by trial) who has no reason to be ashamed, accurately handling and skillfully teaching the Word of Truth."*
>
> ~**2 TIMOTHY 2:15 AMPLIFIED BIBLE**

Focus on the positive occurrences in your life. Focus on your blessings. For one, if you are reading this writing,

God woke you up this morning with a purpose! Before you fall asleep tonight, think of ten things God has done for you today and write them down. Then, when you awake in the morning, read those, and see how they change your perspective and abandon or allow you to control your fears.

Beware: Fear Causes Doubt

> *"But let him ask in faith, with no doubting, for the one who doubts is like a wave of the sea that is driven and tossed by the wind."*
>
> ~JAMES 1:6 ESV

When we think about or try to understand doubt, the disciple Thomas is a good example. He walked with Jesus for the entire time of His ministry and yet, he was reluctant to believe His return (John 11:16; John 14:3-4; John19:16-30; John 20). Thomas was not worshipping but withdrawing into isolation and putting up walls. He was not willing to draw near without witnessing the reality for himself of Jesus returning without proof. He refused to believe the others about the resurrection of Jesus. Thomas was looked upon as one who had a lack of faith. Perhaps that is true, or maybe he had to experience the truth for himself.

Have you ever struggled like Thomas? Have you ever been hurt or grieved by a loved one so dear that you withdrew and became isolated or bitter? Have you ever searched for the truth even though others told you it is real? We all have a moment where we have to bear our sorrow and look deeply for truth. Thank God Thomas' doubt was temporary.

In the face of doubt, try pondering over these questions:

1. Have I spent consistent time in meditation with God and in His Word? Have I shared my concerns, hurt, and despair with Him?
2. Do I believe that God will not allow me to enter into any trial that He has not made a way for me to endure the outcome and exit? No matter how tough it may seem.
3. Has God ever disappointed or left me? What lens am I looking through?
4. Am I trusting God according to His promises and biblical truth?

Breaking Free and Facing Fear

What keys have you used on your journey to overcome the spirit of fear? Please pray and share them with others around you.

> *"I sought the Lord, and He answered me from all my fears. Those who look to Him are radiant, and their faces shall never be ashamed."*
>
> **~PSALM 34:4-5 ESV**

Fear of failure:

Some of us are afraid to try something new because we may fail. We must believe through Christ we can finish the tasks at hand and have faith in His strength. In truth, we learn from our mistakes and work towards accomplishing our goals. When we have made the transition, we are grateful for the experience of being challenged.

> *"Brethren, I do not count myself to have apprehended; but one thing I do: Forgetting those things which are behind and reaching forward to those things which are ahead, I press*

toward the goal for the prize of the upward call of God in Christ Jesus."

~PHILIPPIANS 3:13-14 NKJV

Fear of criticism:

Some of us are so afraid of what people will think that we are fearful of trying new challenges. Overcoming the fear of criticism is essential to fulfilling our purpose. Fear of criticism may stem from childhood into adulthood; that is people speaking negativity instead of encouraging us to try.

First admit when we are wrong and work toward correcting our decisions and reaffirming our position. Learn to limit criticism to constructive criticism. Evaluate your perception of it.

"The ear that listens to life-giving reproof will dwell among the wise. Whoever ignores instructions despises himself, but he who listens to reproof gains intelligence. The fear of the Lord is instructions in wisdom, and humility comes before honor."

~PROVERBS 15:31-33 ESV

Fear of rejection:

Some people are reluctant to try out for activities or promotions because they fear being turned down or rejected. We have all been in a position to be rejected some time on our life journey.

In most instances, it is really a normal way of life, but still, we do not like it. However, we can learn from rejection and turn it into a positive outlook. More than anything else, know we have value, and we have worth. God loves His children. We are reminded that Jesus Christ was rejected and went to the Cross.

> *"And if anyone will not receive you or listen to your words, shake off the dust from your feet when you leave that house or town."*
>
> ~MATTHEW 10:14 ESV

> *"He came to His own, and His own people did not receive Him."*
>
> ~JOHN 1:11 ESV

How can we overcome the spirit of fear?

Believe God: Realize we serve an amazing God who promises never to leave us

> **"The LORD is on my side**; I will not fear. What can man do to me?"
>
> ~PSALM 118:6 ES

Identify your fears: God will empower you to embrace your fears and to call them out. We can step out of our comfort zone and try something different. We can move forward in faith.

Trust God: A bumper sticker once read "Every opportunity to fear is also an opportunity to trust God." When we are fearful, we are powerless but when we give it all to God, we are strengthened by His power.

> "Set your minds on things that are above, not on things that are on earth."
>
> ~COLOSSIANS 3:2 ESV

> *"When I am afraid, I will trust in You. In God, whose Word I praise, In God I trust; I will not be afraid. What can mortal man do to me?*
>
> **~PSALM 56:4 NIV**

Analyze your fear: Think about the fear and get to the root cause of it. Ask God to reveal what is causing your fear and ask Him to help you become delivered from it.

Seek the peace of God: With fear comes torment, calamity, chaos, conflict, and instability. Fear causes our heart to be in turmoil. How can we extinguish fear in our heart? We can do this by seeking the peace of God. Peace comes from having God in our life. Peace comes from the assurance that God is always in control, and He can cast away fear from our heart. Remain humble and compassionate.

Jesus said,

> *"Peace I leave with you; My peace I give you. I do not give to you as the world gives. Do not let your heart be troubled and do not be afraid."*
>
> **~JOHN 14:27 NIV**

Love Conquers All:

To get rid of fear, we must replace it with something more meaningful and in-depth. When love prevails, fear must flee. As long as we have love in our hearts and lives, we can expect fear not to linger, and we can be set free. The moment our love waivers, fear will creep back into our lives. Speak words of love about yourself, the people around you, and your life.

> _"There is no fear in love; but perfect love casts out fear..."_
>
> ~1 JOHN 4:18 ESV

> _"Fighting Spiritual Warfare with the Word of God!_
>
> _"It's a Fixed Fight and We already won!"_
>
> ~JABARI JOHNSON

References taken from:

➤ www.becoming Christian.com
➤ Tony robbins.com/stories/unleash the power/overcoming fear-5-steps

MY GRACE IS SUFFICIENT FOR YOU, FOR MY POWER IS MADE PERFECT IN WEAKNESS.

2ND CORINTHIANS 12:9 NKJV

CHAPTER 9:

COPING WITH CANCER

WHAT OUR FAMILY AND FRIENDS NEED TO KNOW!

The National Coalition for Cancer Survivorship (NCCS) defines a survivor as any person diagnosed with cancer from the time of diagnosis until his or her death. In 1986, the NCCS established an organization to change the societal thought from cancer victim to cancer survivor. In doing so, cancer recovery and experience have changed.

Sometimes, it can really be challenging to talk with cancer survivors. Unless you have been there, you cannot understand what a cancer survivor feels or what they are going through. Years ago, people suffered in silence with their cancer. Ashamed to speak the unspeakable, "I have cancer." Many died without the proper treatment. Education awareness and medical research have pivoted the disease to the forefront of the minds and hearts of everyone.

Today, some people still find it hard to speak to anyone about their experience with cancer. Each cancer survivor has their own story to tell. Listening to them share their story in their own time is the best way to help a cancer survivor get through the traumatic pain and isolation of cancer. The cancer experience is not just physical but also mental and even spiritual. Cancer survivors have a range of emotions, and sometimes just giving them their space can be a tremendous support. Allow them time to share their feelings and give them the freedom to decide what to share without judgment. Let them know you are there when they need you.

Cancer affects all of us in different ways. There are physical and emotional changes that occur with cancer. Some cancer survivors: Lose their hair, lose their nails, lose their skin color, cannot taste, lose their appetite, and are sensitive to touch. Others feel like they are losing their mind and battle feelings of depression, anxiety, and suicide.

Economically cancer can be devastating to a person. Statistical reports have shown that the financial costs of cancer are high for the individual as well as society worldwide. Some cannot work in their profession or secure a decent living. Some have limited or no insurance coverage. Life, liberty, and the pursuit of happiness seem to be distant memories for some cancer survivors. To add to this, racism in healthcare disproportionately affects people of color and causes distrust of the medical field.

If it had not been for my faith, family, and friends, cancer would have been a deeper burden than I dare to imagine bearing. My faith gave me hope and a way to seek purpose in my life. I share this faith, hope, and love with cancer survivors I meet and grow to know.

Faith, Hope, and Love!

We all can show cancer survivors that they are loved and have hope. Most of all, we can let them know through our actions that they are not alone. We can offer encouragement with prayers, soothing music for meditation, running errands, giving them hugs, telephone calls, visits at home and the hospital, and presenting them with inspirational books and gifts of love. We can surround them with kindness, NOT pity. Above all, do not tell them how their treatment should be conducted. That is between God, their family, their physician, and the cancer survivor, NOT you! Please respect their privacy. Be honest with them about your feelings, but remember, it is not about you.

God is the center and a constant presence in our lives. My soul cries out that we have a sincere longing for hope in Jesus Christ. We are merely His messengers. God will change all that needs to be changed in His perfect timing and love. Do what He asks you to do for cancer survivors, not what you think should be done.

Today, with the mercies of God, Cattleya Foundation of Hope can keep the light burning in our hearts and in our actions for the victorious life of cancer survivors. We are a chosen people of God ready to serve and willing to share

His love and compassion. We remain humble and seek God for strength to continue to fight for the right to life.

CHAPTER 10:

WHAT YOU SHOULD KNOW ABOUT CANCER

———— ༄ ༄ ༄ ————

I would like to include these facts I researched on the University of Houston MD Anderson Cancer website. I believe they will be helpful to you as you contemplate your personal decision and how to prepare for your life journey and need to make life changing decisions. I pray this information will help you if you are faced with the decision of the best treatment for breast cancer. Ask as many questions as you need and listen carefully to what is being told to you. Be sure to go to your appointment with a pen and paper so you can take notes and review them when you are at home.

What is a Mastectomy?

According to the website, a mastectomy is one of the treatment methods for breast cancer. It is a breast cancer surgery in which the surgeon removes the tumor and the entire breast. But not every breast cancer patient needs this surgery. MD Anderson performs approximately 550 of these surgeries annually.

Types of Mastectomies:

➢ **Total mastectomy:** The surgeon removes the entire breast and most of the overlying skin.

➢ **Partial mastectomy:** This is also called a lumpectomy. In this procedure, the surgeon removes the tumor and surrounding breast tissue.

➢ **Radical mastectomy:** The surgeon removes the breast tissue and surrounding chest muscles. This was once the most common type of mastectomy, but it is rarely performed today.

➤ **Modified radical mastectomy:** The surgeon removes the breast tissue and lymph nodes under the arm to remove cancer and indicate how far the cancer has spread.

➤ **Nipple-sparing mastectomy:** The surgeon removes all of the breast tissue but leaves the nipples and the areola.

➤ **Skin-sparing mastectomy**: The surgeon removes all of the breast tissue, including the nipple and areola, but leaves the skin.

➤ **Double mastectomy**: Also called a bilateral mastectomy, this is when the surgeon removes the tissue from both breasts. A double mastectomy is performed if there is cancer in both breasts or if the patient has a BRCA 1 or BRCA 2 genetic mutation, which raises the risk of cancer.

Who needs a Mastectomy?

According to the website information the following candidates will undergo this type of surgery.

Because the mastectomy is so well-known, breast cancer patients often assume that is the treatment they should have or will have to have. But well-established research going back to the 1970s shows that, together, patients who have a lumpectomy and radiation therapy have the same low risk of breast cancer recurrence as patients who have a mastectomy.

Mastectomies are best for patients who cannot withstand radiation. This includes patients who:

➢ had radiation therapy previously,

➢ have a recurrent cancer, or

➢ have soft-tissue disorders.

Mastectomies are also a good option if the patient is not a lumpectomy candidate based on the size or location of the breast cancer.

"When I meet with a patient, I like to give them all the options and discuss which one is safest for them," Suzie Sun MD says. "Ultimately, I want the patients to choose what treatment is best for them."

What are the risks of a mastectomy?

Like any surgery, a mastectomy has some risks. These include:

> **Breast pain**

> **Swelling**

> **Necrosis:** If the patient has a nipple-sparing or skin-sparing mastectomy, there is some risk that the skin will not receive enough blood and need to be removed.

What should patients expect during a mastectomy?

Before a mastectomy, patients receive general anesthesia. The surgery typically takes about two hours but may take longer if the surgeon needs to remove any surrounding lymph nodes to determine whether the cancer has spread, or if the patient plans to undergo breast reconstruction.

How long does it take to recover from a mastectomy?

Patients who do not undergo reconstruction typically leave the hospital the next day. Patients who have breast reconstruction using their own tissue and a mastectomy are typically in the hospital a little longer – about four to five days.

Patients who have additional reconstruction along with a mastectomy will need more time to recover, depending on which type of breast reconstruction they choose.

What types of breast reconstruction are available for patients who have had a mastectomy?

Breast cancer patients who have undergone a mastectomy have many options for breast reconstruction. A plastic surgeon will meet with you to discuss which options are best for you.

These options include the following: implant reconstruction or reconstruction using the patient's own tissue. Both options may be done immediately or may be delayed.

This article was updated on June 4, 2021, by Kellie Bramlet Blackburn. [2]

According to the National Cancer Institute, here are some questions you may want to ask your physician during and after your cancer treatment.

"When you have finished your cancer treatment, you will talk with your doctor about next steps and follow-up care. You may want to ask your doctor some of the following questions:

> ➤ How long will it take for me to get better and feel more like myself?
> ➤ What kind of care should I expect after my treatment?
> ➤ What long-term health issues can I expect as a result of my cancer and its treatment?
> ➤ What is the chance that my cancer will return?
> ➤ What symptoms should I tell you about?
> ➤ Who do I call if I develop these symptoms?
> ➤ What can I do to be as healthy as possible?

---

[2] www.mdanderson.org/cancerwise/whatisamastectomy.html

➤ Which doctor(s) should I see for my follow-up care? How often?

➤ What tests do I need after treatment is over? How often will I have the tests?

➤ What records do I need to keep about my treatment?

➤ Is there a counselor I can talk to or an online or in-person support group you can suggest?"

Disparities in Health Care Among People of Color

According to the National Cancer Institute (NCI), "tremendous progress has been made against cancer thanks to decades of investment in cancer research. However, certain groups still bear a disproportionate burden of cancer compared with others. We cannot make the progress needed to end cancer as we know it if segments of the population are not included.

The National Cancer Institute and other medical organizations have begun to take a deeper look since COVID at the disparities in treatment for cancer patients among Black people, Hispanics, and people of Ethnic backgrounds.

"Equity, diversity, and inclusion (EDI) are core values at NCI, and the institute has **conducted and supported research on cancer disparities** for decades.

However, the events of the summer of 2020, including incidents of violence against people of color and other minority communities and the nationwide protests that followed, have prompted many organizations to take a hard look at how structural racism affects how they work.

And the disproportionate and alarming impact COVID-19 has had on people of color and other minority communities is evidence that more work must be done to end health disparities.

Social determinants of health, workforce discrimination, and unfair hiring practices all play a role in perpetuating health inequities. And while NCI has always been committed to fairness and addressing health, we are now focused on identifying and eliminating the impact of deep-rooted structural racism that has hampered progress.

NCI, like **the rest of NIH**, (National Institute of Health) is taking a stand to address and eventually end structural racism within the biomedical community".

I can see the move of God to change the minds and change the hearts of the medical professionals who have taken an oath to ensure the medical health and wholeness of everyone they serve.

Standing Together in Christ!

THE TIME IS NOW!

"GREET ONE ANOTHER
WITH A HOLY KISS"

———

PSALM 102:1-2 ESV

"GREET ONE ANOTHER WITH THE
KISS OF LOVE AND PEACE BE WITH
YOU IN CHRIST JESUS"

———

1 PETER 5:14 ESV

CHAPTER 11:

FOR THE WARRIORS: LIFE AFTER CANCER

———— ༂༂༂ ————

Now that you are a cancer survivor or a thriver, how are you living your life differently?

I must ask the question resonating in the minds and thoughts of many Christian women, "What is the true meaning of my life in today's world?" For me, I am not defined by cancer or this world but by living my life as a humble servant believing in the power of Jesus Christ. Knowing He loves me and gave His life for me. Every day holds the possibility of a new miracle.

As Christian women, we face many complexities and challenges in this world. How do we cope with these challenges in our lives? Our journey may draw us in different directions, such as family, career, personal goals, education, pursuit of relationships, health issues, church, ministry, and God. Yet, we are still Christian women yearning to please our God and raise our children. We are determined to live a full and meaningful life filled with love and great aspirations.

When faced with decisions beyond the realm of our capabilities, through faith in God, the impossible is possible and the power of prayer will prevail. When the storms come, and all seems dim in our lives, we know that we can do all things through Christ who strengthens us. We have a Savior who has promised us in His Word and with His life that He will comfort us in our circumstances and trials in this world. God promised us a new life in Jesus Christ. Our heads are held high and looking to the hills from whence cometh our help. In Christ Jesus, we are stronger than we know, and we can accomplish greatness. Cancer cannot stop our purpose and our destiny.

I am reminded of the story of the woman with the issue of blood revealed in Matthew 9:20, Mark 5:24-34, and

Luke 8:42-48. As the story unfolds, the people were crowding around Jesus with great curiosity and anticipation of healing and a miracle. The crowd was pushing, shoving, and trying to make their way to Jesus. Jairus, a ruler in the Synagogue, risked everything, humbled himself, pushed through the crowd, and fell at Jesus' feet, begging Him to help his dying twelve-year-old daughter.

As Jesus begins the journey to help this little girl, there is a woman with an issue of blood who was reaching for Him. This woman had been bleeding for twelve years. She had been seen by many doctors, and no doubt had been given various types of medicine to help her condition. She probably had depleted all of her money seeking a cure. Her condition was worsening, and she was dying. One day she heard of Jesus walking through her city. She made a choice to seek Him. "If only I can touch the hem of His garment." She struggled to touch him. She was in a hopeless situation and reaching for a miracle.

Have you ever been in a situation where you thought there was no way out? Perhaps it was a negative doctor's report, and you were told you have cancer, a family tragedy or one of your children is in great trouble. What do you do? Who do you turn to for help? How do you cope? In biblical days, she was considered unclean, and anyone or thing that touched her would be uncleaned (Leviticus 15:25-27).

Yet, she pushed through the crowd anyway. She was determined and refused to give up. Finally, she reached the hem of Jesus' garment, and immediately she was healed. Jesus felt power leave Him, and He turned with a question, "Who touched Me?" Of course, the disciples had no idea! The woman came forward shivering in fear and confessed the truth to Jesus. His reply to her was, "Daughter, go in peace and be freed from your suffering. Your faith has made you whole." The woman was given a new identity by Jesus. He called her "daughter," not "the woman with the issue of blood". Her faith got His attention, and He was moved with compassion to show her mercy. Jesus' power healed both Jairus' little girl and the woman with the issue of blood because they believed.

As we share our stories, we are telling everyone what magnitude God will take to come to the aid of His child. We are living witnesses of God's miracles! We can show the world how our faith in Christ will overcome any obstacles in our way. We are victorious in Christ Jesus.

Mary, the Mother of Jesus Christ, was a poor young virgin girl, which in her day would have made her seem an unlikely candidate for any major task for God. Nevertheless, God chose Mary for the most important act of obedience that He had at that time asked of anyone. You may think your body riddled with sickness, lack of education, limited skills, a small number of abilities or experience, or simply the fact that you are a woman makes you an unlikely candidate for the service of God. Do not limit God or His choice to choose you for His purpose. He can use you if you trust Him. Believe in the power of Jesus Christ in all circumstances, and your faith will change your situation.

God promised Mary that she would bear the Son of God. Mary's submission to God led to our salvation. When sorrow weighs me down and dims my hope, I think of Mary and the woman with the issue of blood. I have learned to wait patiently for God to finish working His plan for my life. Impossibilities become possibilities through faith in Jesus Christ. In every situation that exists, God is in control. Even though we may face humanly impossible circumstances, we are mindful that God can do the impossible. Our response to His commands should not be laughter, fear, or doubt, but willing acceptance of the mission and journey.

God's purpose was for the Son of God to face the consequences of sin in the world through His innocence and ultimate death. He needed "One" who was sinless to carry forth His plan through His blood sacrifice. Jesus Christ was the only one who could restore fellowship between God and humanity. Scriptures teach us that life is in the blood. It took Jesus' blood to restore our life with God, our Father.

All my life I have had to struggle against impossibilities. People looked at me and saw the color of my skin, but against all odds, through Christ, my impossibilities became possibilities. People have looked at me and said, "You are a woman; you cannot possibly accomplish this endeavor," but against all odds, my impossibilities became possibilities through Jesus Christ. People looked at me and said, "You are too little and timid; you can never accomplish anything worthwhile," but against all odds, my impossibilities became possibilities. No, cancer was not going to stop me, and I implore you to fight for your own life. Do not give up! My strength comes from my Lord and Savior, Jesus Christ, and nothing is impossible for my God!

I am grateful to God for calling me into evangelism and allowing me the humble privilege of sharing the good news of Jesus Christ with the world on this journey. The road may not always be easy or fair but sharing the love of God with the sick, downtrodden, homeless, and destitute is reward enough. Just to witness God working in their lives is immensely encouraging to me. Thank You, Jesus, for the Perfect example that You have taught us with your life, death, and resurrection. Can we wash the feet of our brother or sister? Can we offer grace to our sister or our brother with unconditional love? Faith without works is dead (James 2:14-26 NKJV). There is nothing we can do to get into Heaven because Jesus paid the ultimate price with His life. Will you accept His gift of salvation?

Chosen!

> BLESSED BE THE GOD AND FATHER OF OUR LORD JESUS CHRIST, THE FATHER OF MERCIES AND GOD OF ALL COMFORT, 4 WHO COMFORTS US IN ALL OUR AFFLICTION, SO THAT WE MAY BE ABLE TO COMFORT THOSE WHO ARE IN ANY AFFLICTION, WITH THE COMFORT WITH WHICH WE OURSELVES ARE COMFORTED BY GOD. 5 FOR AS WE SHARE ABUNDANTLY IN CHRIST'S SUFFERINGS, SO THROUGH CHRIST WE SHARE ABUNDANTLY IN COMFORT TOO.[A] 6 IF WE ARE AFFLICTED, IT IS FOR YOUR COMFORT AND SALVATION; AND IF WE ARE COMFORTED, IT IS FOR YOUR COMFORT, WHICH YOU EXPERIENCE WHEN YOU PATIENTLY ENDURE THE SAME SUFFERINGS THAT WE SUFFER.

2 CORINTHIANS 1:3-6 ESV

CHAPTER 12:

A SURVIVOR'S TESTIMONY

This is my personal interview with Teresa Cole, a Bilateral Breast Cancer Survivor from Abundant Love Fellowship Church, Hewitt, Texas.

One morning the phone rang, and when I answered the call, it was Sis Teresa Cole. The conversations between us in the past have always been joyful and pleasant. However, today our conversation was troubling. She had received disturbing news about her health, and her mind was overwhelmed. The Holy Spirit led her to speak with me. She feared what her future would look like and needed to talk with someone she felt would understand. She knows I am a breast cancer survivor and that I am a part of Cattleya. It's common for those with a cancer diagnosis to seek another cancer survivor to bear their intimate thoughts.

"Good morning, Sis Cole. How are you?" I asked.

"Good morning, Dr. Henry. Not well," she responded.

"Oh? What's wrong?" I asked.

"I just received a diagnosis from my doctor, and I have breast cancer."

"Teresa, you still have hope in Jesus Christ, and He will fight for you the same way He fought for me. You are not alone, and we will walk together," I reassured.

At this point, I listened and let her share her thoughts and feelings with me. She shared with me these words, "I want to live!" Teresa chose to have a bilateral mastectomy. This is the surgical removal of both breasts to work toward preventing cancer from recurring. She realized she was at high risk for cancer to return. She had close family members who were cancer survivors and an aunt who died due to her breast cancer returning.

This is Teresa Cole's testimony of her breast cancer journey.

"My breast cancer journey started two years ago. My primary doctor found a small growth that she felt needed to be observed. Every six months, I had to have a mammogram to ensure it was not growing. In October 2021, I thought I was having my last six-month mammogram, but the technician called me back and stated I needed an ultrasound.

The test confirmed the doctor's suspicion. The area of concern was beginning to grow, and I needed a biopsy to determine if it was cancerous. On October 30, 2021, I was scheduled for a biopsy. On November 5, 2021, I was at home talking with a relative when I received the call that the testing was positive for breast cancer. The nurse navigator from Providence Cancer Center told me I needed to discuss treatment. I would be scheduled to speak with an oncologist (a doctor who specializes in cancer), and my primary doctor would help me with the appointment. We would also discuss meeting with a surgeon.

I was not depressed at first, but my primary doctor knew I suffered from anxiety, and she prescribed me some anxiety medication. I was afraid because several of my family members had suffered from cancer, and my family history of cancer is high. Our family is a good candidate for genetic testing, and I also decided to have those tests done. I watched my aunt battle breast cancer and saw it return in her. She died of breast cancer.

My oncologist was very thorough in explaining what was happening and showed me the breast tests and where the cancer was located. He also explained the treatment that was available for me. My option was a lumpectomy with radiation or a mastectomy. I also met with a plastic surgeon for reconstructive surgery. I had considered delayed reconstructive surgery, but I proceeded at the doctor's recommendation.

This is where things took a turn and began to change in my treatment. I was having difficulty contacting the surgeon that was recommended. His office staff was not returning my phone calls. I spoke to the plastic surgeon again in hopes she would have better contact. I had decided to have a bilateral mastectomy with delayed reconstruction by this time. I tried another avenue of contact, sent a message through the patient portal, and requested a call. I kept thinking about how much time was passing without the proper medical treatment for my condition. Faith and prayer were constant in my life, and I clung to God's word through this ordeal. I prayed to God for healing, and others prayed with me too.

Finally, I met with the surgeon. His mannerism towards my decision to have a bilateral mastectomy was daunting, and I felt he was not helpful. I felt like he did not want me as a patient. I was in tears over this trauma. I felt I was at risk. I became more uneasy as I thought about the battles women in my family fought with cancer. I saw the effects of radiation treatment with them and did not want that. My son noticed the change taking place. He said to me, "Mom, you look grayish! You are not smiling the same." He was concerned about what this was doing to me.

I prayed and asked God to help me decide. I lost trust in my surgeon. With my husband by my side, I decided to have a second opinion. I contacted Baylor Scott and White Hillcrest Medical Center – McClinton Cancer Center in Waco, Texas. I was scheduled to see the surgeon on January 27, 2022. On February 11, 2022, I had a bilateral mastectomy. I became concerned about what I would put my body through with reconstructive surgery. How would my body react to the silicone? Would I have an allergic reaction? I am a diabetic and had to think about the recovery time and healing. After everything I had been through, I decided against the delayed reconstructive surgery.

I have a younger sister, Crystal, who lives in San Jose California. She is with an organization that knits bra inserts for breast cancer survivors called Knitted Knockers. They donate them to cancer patients. My sister sent me a box of these Knitted Knockers, and when I saw them, they helped me to feel even more confident about my reconstructive surgery decision. I am thankful for my life. God made breasts for us to nurture and care for our children naturally. They do not define who I am!

Today, I am glad I had the bilateral mastectomy. Now I can sleep without worries or fears about this trauma. My scars are still healing, and the lymph nodes seem to be the hardest to heal. However, I did not have to have chemotherapy or radiation. I look in the mirror and feel gratitude that God is with me and took care of me. Some people have expressed sorrow to me, but the alternative was life or death! God knew my pain, and I trusted Him to see me through.

To women who may be beginning your journey, I say to you, there will be peaks and valleys along your journey, but God is already there and will give you direction. Remember, you can ask for a second opinion. I did not ask, "Why me" because I believed in God. I chose to cut my hair in case I had to undergo chemotherapy and anticipate hair loss. The support of all the women and breast cancer survivors stopped me from feeling alone."

Thank you, Sis. Cole, for your intimate and compelling story of faith that you have shared with us. We celebrate with those who have survived the trauma of cancer. Testimonies like this are an inspiration for those who have been diagnosed with cancer. There is proof we can continue our life journeys after cancer. This is an example to the world of what life after cancer looks like when you walk with Christ.

> *Blessed be the God and Father of our Lord Jesus Christ, the Father of mercies and God of all comfort, 4 Who comforts us in all our affliction, so that we may be able to comfort those who are in any affliction, with the comfort with which we ourselves are comforted by God. 5 For as we share abundantly in Christ's sufferings, so through Christ we share abundantly in comfort too.[a] 6 If we are afflicted, it is for your comfort and salvation; and if we are comforted, it is for your comfort, which You experience when You patiently endure the same sufferings that we suffer.*
>
> **(2 CORINTHIANS 1:3-6 ESV)**

CARE FOR THE FLOCK THAT GOD HAS ENTRUSTED YOU. WATCH OVER IT, WILLINGLY, NOT GRUDGINGLY, NOT FOR WHAT YOU WILL GET OUT OF IT, BUT BECAUSE YOU ARE EAGER TO SERVE GOD.

———

1PETER 5:2 NLT

CHAPTER 13:

CATTLEYA FOUNDATION OF HOPE

———— ༄ ༄ ༄ ————

CHANGING LIVES – RESTORING HOPE

> *"I pray that God, the Source of Hope, will fill you completely with joy and peace because you trust in Him. Then you will overflow with confident hope through the power of the Holy Spirit."*
>
> ~ROMANS 15:13 NLT

WALKING IN FAITH
(Our Purpose and Mission)

As I began to ruminate over my victorious battle with cancer, my heart was thankful to those who shared so much love with me. The Holy Spirit showered me with the gift of love and compassion through the hearts of others. I remember asking Him, "what can I do for those who chose to love me through the suffering and emotional agony of cancer?" He spoke to me in a way that changed my life forever. "You can never repay love; you can only pay it forward!"

God was about to reveal to me my purpose and mission. I was going to share my battle with cancer and my fight for life with the world. As a result, Cattleya was born! This is my missional journey with the Holy Spirit leading the way.

> "And now abide faith, hope, and love, these three; but the greatest of these is love."
>
> ~1 CORINTHIANS 13:13 NKJV

A Celebration of Life

On Saturday, August 29, 2015, God permitted me to host "A Celebration of Life" luncheon at the Spa at Canyon Oaks in Crawford, Texas. It's a beautiful spa resort nestled on thirty-one acres of land with weekend and overnight cottages. It was a place I often visited to relax and leave the city behind. I love to relax there and have a facial, massage, shop, and a healthy lunch. I would often sit outside with my book and enjoy the beauty of nature surrounding the grounds. The staff was always so friendly and welcoming.

This place where I had created so many memories would also be the place I would fulfill my purpose. I believe God prepares us for His plan and our future endeavors innocently. Have you ever spoken these words, "God was preparing me all this time, and I did not realize it until He revealed His plan to me?" Well, that's how I felt. When God gave me the vision of the launch of the celebration, I imagined a few friends, family members, cancer survivors, and associates would celebrate the humble chapter of my life with me. It has often been expressed that if you want God to laugh, tell Him your plans.

Once the invitations began to circulate and the word spread, I received so many calls from people who wanted to participate. Eventually, the spa had to inform me that they were at capacity and could not facilitate any more guests. It truly hurt me to have to deny entrance to even one person! Love flows from breast to breast and from heart to heart, and this celebration was all about love. God knew exactly where we all needed to be that day and who should attend. He appointed me as His vessel to bring us on a life-changing journey.

As I continued to prepare for the celebration, my Abundant Love sisters were willing to help coordinate the luncheon. My dear friends, Michelle Hicks and Rev. Dr. Mary Hamilton were instrumental in securing donations to fund some of the costs involved in the luncheon. In addition, each guest was gracious enough to pay for their lunch that day.

Our keynote and motivational speaker was Sister Hattie Mae Black, my dear sister in Christ. I also invited two board members from the Susan G. Komen

Foundation, Jane Allen, and their board president, Ms. Clendendon to attend the luncheon.

The Holy Spirit led me to ask the Komen Foundation participants to share health and wellness information about breast cancer, women's health issues, and prosperity. As women, we need to be educated about the importance of breast self-examination, mammograms, and living a proactive and healthy lifestyle. They spoke and encouraged us to embrace life with hope and gave us all some beautiful bags to remember the occasion that I hold dear today. I still did not completely see God's plan right away, but I truly felt His presence.

On that day, Janice Matthews and I arrived before any other guests and were blessed by each other's company. We were old friends who had been through the whirlwind experience of a battle with cancer. Now we could share our gratefulness to God and love for one another. We laughed, talked, took pictures, had a massage, and enjoyed our time together. Janice shared with me her intimate experience of living without her breast. I had visited Janice during that time but did not understand the emotional, life-changing experience and impact of cancer. I just wanted to be there for my friend. Now we are part of the sisterhood that neither of us would want anyone else ever to join. This was the sisterhood of breast cancer survivors.

Every cancer survivor has a story to tell and how they continue to cope with the challenges of cancer. Janice and I will always have an inseparable bond that links us together forever. I am overjoyed with gratitude that God orchestrated our lives many years ago so that we could care for one another through love. We are victorious through Christ. She is one of my dearest friends, an amazing woman, and a humble servant of our Lord. She is soft-spoken with a beautiful smile. Unfortunately, Janice could not stay for the luncheon that day because she had prior business and work obligations. Thank you, Janice, for answering the call of God and being His messenger in my life.

The hour had come for me to greet my family, cancer survivors, and friends. My heart was filled with gladness and love as they began to arrive. My heart was overflowing with excitement for what God was going to do. That day, we were free to love one another without restraints or unwarranted judgment. We were grateful for our lives, eating and drinking together in fellowship, listening to music to soothe our souls and inspire our hearts. It was a time we all could grasp the opportunity to hear His Voice speaking to us and receive His Wisdom through His Word. God had a purpose and a plan to share with all of us that day. We are a significant and deliberate part of Him and the revelation of His love.

> *"I cry out to God Most High, To God who fulfills His purpose for me."*
>
> ~PSALM 57:2 NKJV

Lord, I am listening. Please continue to speak to me!

God's plan and vision were unfolding in such a miraculous way. I was in awe of His awesomeness. His humility and great love for each of us were being revealed in this special way He created for us to spend time with Him. As God's chosen messenger, my dear sister, Sister Hattie Black, would deliver our Heavenly Father's message that day. What a precious gift from God! When God shared with me who He had chosen to speak His

Word to us, my heart leaped for joy. Sister Hattie is another dear friend and is more like a sister to me. She is certainly a sister in God's Kingdom with a giving heart of faith. We have known each other for many years as we have served in the community, attended church together, and walked together in times of trouble and dismay. We share the mutual feeling of love for God and one another. I am also a witness to her willingness to please Him.

At the event, I was also reminded that we were celebrating the challenges, obstacles, achievements, and triumphs of our lives. Yet, we were embarking on a new journey filled with hope and a purpose. Sister Hattie brought a beautiful Word from the Lord about who we are as women. His message reminded me that we are humble, giving, compassionate, busy, nurturing, selfless women who sacrifice a lot for others without asking for anything in return. At times, we are too busy to see to our own needs, desires, and care. Sometimes we must stop and clearly hear from God the direction He chooses for our lives. Sister Hattie inspired us to lift our heads and embrace life with the love of God. She empowered us through the word of God to encourage one another and to seek Him in all things. She asked us to pledge to care for each other and pray for one another.

Dear Sister Hattie brought a beautiful handmade framed gift for me that I still cherish today. What I love most about this heartfelt gift is that it tells the story of my life journey after cancer artistically. It was truly fitting for the occasion, and it instructed me where God would lead next. As I looked around the room at everyone, I saw the eagerness of souls willing to receive God's love, letting go of personal baggage and self-doubt that was weighing them down. I witnessed a clear move of women and their desires to please and reverence God. At that moment, we were firmly planted on a life journey to walk in faith. We committed to trusting God along the path, expanding our minds, opening our hearts, exploring innovative ideas, and believing in the power of the Holy Spirit to lead us in everything we do to serve the Lord.

Some of the women participants expressed their joy in attending and hoped that we would gather together again in the future. They expressed their gratitude for educating them on breast cancer statistics and what they needed to do to keep living. Others were grateful to share their stories with sisters who would listen and encourage their spirit. I knew that would not be the only time we would celebrate His love. I knew we had work to do, and we had to share that moment with others.

At that moment, I knew His Will for my life journey. I received His vision and said 'yes' to God and His will. That celebration was for the Glory of God.

> "For we are His workmanship, created in Christ Jesus for good works, which God prepared beforehand that we should walk in them.
>
> ~EPHESIANS 2:20 NKJV

Celebrate Him with Love!

Shelia Ross was among the people that attended the "A Celebration of Life" luncheon. After the luncheon, I was led by the Holy Spirit to approach her with the vision God had shared with me. You see, I realized the people attending this luncheon were there for a purpose. The luncheon was just the beginning of God's purpose and plan for our lives. We were all given a mission that day to do the will of God. To go forth, serve the people in our communities and the world, and obey His command outlined in the great Commission (Matthew 28:16-20 NKJV). Our purpose and forecast were to live life with great expectations.

Shelia and I talked about continuing the work that started at the luncheon. As we spoke to one another, God's plan continued to unfold. We knew we were to seek His wisdom even though He had not fully revealed His purpose to us. We knew the Holy Spirit would give us direction. We knew faith, prayers, and trusting God were the keys to His blessings for the future. We also knew that we needed to involve other people and believed God would provide all our needs for His mission. Our hearts were in step to serve and please God. Our minds were clear. This was God's vision, and our ears needed to listen for His Voice.

It was imperative that we sought spiritual guidance as we embarked on the journey. Pastor Edward L. Ross, Senior Pastor of Abundant Love Fellowship Church, was willing to be there for us. We asked Pastor Ross to pray for us, and without hesitation, he did. Pastor Ross is a visionary pastor, and under his leadership and teaching, his church strives to share the love of Christ with everyone and meet the needs of people. No matter who they are or what their past looks like, or their walk of life. I am blessed and thankful to be a member partner. I can freely worship God and work on deepening my relationship with Him without restraints or bias. I love the people of Abundant Love and their willingness to please God. We aim to "try something different" through the love of Christ. We are not perfect but strive to be like Christ. If you are striving to build a Christian ministry, organization, or foundation, seek God for its development and maturation; ask him for the spiritual leader He wants to cover you as you serve Him.

It was also important that Cattleya pursued community involvement and support for us to move forward. I approached Catherine Bauer, coordinator of Leadership Plenty Institute of America, of which I am a graduate. She introduced me to Jamie Goble, who was instrumental in assisting us in obtaining our 501C3 nonprofit status through the Internal Revenue Service. I am grateful for the friendship that blossomed between Jamie and me through this endeavor. I contacted the Secretary's and the Comptroller's Offices for further details on submitting the proper forms, the certificate of formation, and the Articles of Incorporation. Keisha Bridges-Miller was instrumental in establishing the 990N Form for the Internal Revenue Service as our tax consultant. Thank You, God, for building the collaboration of community partners and Cattleya.

Jane Allen is a thirteen-year breast cancer survivor, and we are both devoted to fighting cancer and passionate about serving our communities together. Since our first introduction at the luncheon, Jane Allen has always been willing to lend a helping hand to Cattleya in so many ways. Jane has been willing to reach out to her associates on behalf of Cattleya, which has been essential to our growth. As our relationship has grown into an endearing one over the years, I am thankful to God for bringing us together. It is amazing how through circumstances, God places people in our lives to share loving experiences and lasting memories at just the right time. Thank you, Jane, for your love and friendship. The purpose of God is etched into the depth of our service permanently.

God's Vision and Plan

> "Be anxious for nothing, but in everything by prayer and supplication, with thanksgiving, let your requests be made known to God, and the peace of God, which surpasses all understanding, will guard your hearts and minds through Christ Jesus. Finally, brethren, whatever things are true, whatever things are noble, whatever things are just, whatever things are pure, whatever things are lovely, whatever things are of good report, if there is any virtue and if there is anything praiseworthy, meditate on these things. The things which you learned and received and heard and saw in Me, these do, and the God of peace will be with you."
>
> ~PHILIPPIANS 4:6-9 NKJV

> "I beseech you therefore, brethren, by the mercies of God, that you present your bodies a living sacrifice, holy, acceptable to God, which is your reasonable service. And do not conform to this world, but be transformed by the renewing of

your mind, that you may prove what is that good and acceptable and perfect will of God."

~ROMANS 12:1-2 NKJV

On February 15, 2016, I met with Shelia, Lisa (a colon cancer survivor and registered nurse), Toria (a breast cancer survivor and registered nurse), and Sandra (a registered nurse) at Panera Bread, one of my favorite lunch spots. Our purpose was to begin to work together to continue the vision given by God at the "*A Celebration of Life*" luncheon and to establish a cancer foundation in McLennan County. I really did not know any of them on a personal level but trusted God. So, how do we put our talk into action? How do we establish a Christian foundation? How do we find compatible interests and work together to serve God? How do we draw on the strengths of each other for His service? Clearly, He had outlined our mission and put us on the right road.

Our mission was to love and respect one another, serve cancer survivors, and give them hope in Christ Jesus. The Holy Spirit was leading the way and continues to guide us today. It is our choice to be obedient to Him and follow His direction. James 2:26 says, "Faith without works is dead." Paul said, "For we walk by faith and not by sight." We developed a strategic plan to face the enormous challenges that were ahead of us. We would be held accountable for the assignment each of us was given.

We began to step out on faith, and established a name, Cattleya Foundation of Hope. A Cattleya board was established with the five of us as founding members; we developed bylaws, and later governing policies and procedures were adapted for the growth and future of the foundation. As a foundation, we are still governed by these laws today. We chose the Cattleya orchid as the emblem for its strength, beauty, grace, and viability, and the colors purple, gold, and ivory as a distinct way to identify our foundation.

We have included these colors, their representation, and the orchid permanently into our bylaws as a reminder of our specific purpose and mission. We also adopted the following core values into the fabric of Cattleya: compassion, commitment, courage, communication, excellence, accountability, service, and integrity.

When we began our journey, we had no financial investors to help us become incorporated, file for nonprofit status, or set up business or banking. We looked to our Source, God, and He made it possible for us to become our own financial investors! We did not have office space, but we needed a place for the Cattleya board and our membership to conduct business meetings. So, initially, Shelia and I alternated our homes for meetings. God led me to ask the Cooper House Foundation if they would be able to accommodate the needs of our board meetings. We pray for a place where we can increase our ability to serve the cancer survivor community. We continue to patiently wait on the will of God.

Everything we have done has been because of our Lord and Savior, Jesus Christ. He knows when we will be ready to move to the next level of ministry. We thank You, Lord, and remain humble and content in service to You. Through continuous prayers, we join in faith to plant seeds of hope in cancer survivors, witnessing the transformation of their lives, and we continue to let them know they are not alone on their journey. God has blessed our membership to grow to twenty members, and we meet at the Good Neighbor Settlement House or at Pastor Ruby Minnit's church, Greater Love, both in Waco, Texas, who is also a Cattleya member.

Cattleya is God's vision, and He commands us to care for cancer survivors according to His plan on their life journey. As we approach like-minded Christian friends and family willing to support cancer survivors, we must be mindful of who God chooses for His mission. After all, I believe that was the purpose of the luncheon at Canyon Oaks. I heard God clearly speaking to me. Have you ever heard the voice of God whisper in your ear and your whole life changed forever? It is such a fantastic experience!

I believe if God tells you to go, He will provide for you in His plan, and everything will work according to His timing. Trusting and believing in Him through our faith is the essential component of the work and mission of Cattleya.

In May 2016, we began to plan our next "A Celebration of Life" fundraising event. It would continue through the history of Cattleya in the month of August. Jane Allen was instrumental in helping us to secure the facility at Castle Heights Bijoux Event Center. The board members and cancer survivors' pictures were displayed on the outside of the facility in window boxes, which was another way to advertise the foundation.

Shelia did a beautiful job designing our flyer and tickets that circulated throughout the city and beyond to bring awareness to the event and to Cattleya. The event had to attract the community and its cancer survivors for our existence. God blessed us with nearly one hundred participants from across Central Texas for that night. We gave small gifts to each of the cancer survivors in attendance, a tradition that we plan to continue at every function and fellowship for survivors today. God keeps His promises, and we must be obedient to recognize our cancer survivors and their journey!

Our keynote speaker for the evening was Cindy Janecka, LCSW, and her twelve-year-old daughter, Courtney, played her guitar. Cindy is a breast cancer survivor, international motivational speaker, and writer. She has written several books about her fight with breast cancer and her mother's death to inspire and encourage other survivors about life after cancer. In addition, Courtney has been making and selling bracelets since she was nine years old to help support their mission.

The proceeds went toward Cindy being able to provide her books to hospitals, churches, and cancer centers without cost, to give hope to cancer survivors. They were both amazing, and God showered us with His love through both of them. Our audience was so grateful for their words and music of encouragement that they dubbed them the "Dynamic Duo." Later that evening, Cindy and I spoke for a few minutes, and she left me with a seed from the Lord that I continue to cherish in my heart, *"And we know that all things work together for good to those who love God, to those who are the called according to His purpose" (Romans 8:28 NKJV).* Since that time, Cindy and I have become dear friends and keep in touch with one another. I thank God for blessing me with her friendship and sharing her with us that night.

Courtney gave me two of her bracelets which I still have to this day. Cattleya gave Cindy a beautiful basket chocked full of delights and inspiration designed by Lisa and Toria. Our mission was accomplished that evening, and we set the atmosphere for Cattleya to connect with the community as far as God would allow us to travel. Mainly we were to connect with cancer survivors. Most of all, we answered God's call to do His will and glorify Him.

We will wait on God, but I can see Cattleya being known on a national level in her future. My God and His Power will determine where we go and who we serve. I am just grateful He called me to be part of this extraordinary gift of life in this ministry.

God's Glory reigns!

Building Community Programs and Outreach

> *"But seek first the Kingdom of God and His righteousness, and all these things shall be added to you."*
>
> ~MATTHEW 6:33 NKJV

It took approximately six to twelve months for Cattleya to be established in the community and recognized through Federal, State, and local government entities, businesses, nonprofits, and organizations as an incorporated Christian cancer foundation. As our membership in Cattleya grew, so did our status in the McLennan County community and sister cities.

I chose to include several of our programs in this writing to give you an idea of how the work of Cattleya was birthed and how God can help you create your programs in your neighborhoods and communities. These programs stretched beyond our local needs and helped us partner with other nonprofits to recognize the needs of cancer survivors in other cities. Sharing these program initiatives with you is a way for you to step out of your comfort zones and make a significant impact in this fight for life. I did it, and you can do it too.

Our focus remained steadfast on establishing programs for Cattleya that would benefit cancer survivor clients. So how did we accomplish these goals? Our first order of business was to introduce ourselves to the medical facilities in McLennan County and the Central Texas area.

Because God blessed us with registered nurses, they spoke with the social workers on our behalf. They contacted Baylor Scott & White Hillcrest Medical Center, McClinton Cancer Center in Waco, Texas, and Baylor Scott & White McLane's Children Hospital in Temple, Texas, about partnering with Cattleya. They reported to the Cattleya board that Temple, Texas, was the nearest cancer facility for children with cancer. The connection was a success. Today, we remain partners with a professional relationship that benefits cancer survivors on their life journey. I encourage you to seek community medical professionals to assist your organization or foundation as they are essential in building community relationships.

Cattleya Transportation Program

In 2016, we developed the Cattleya Transportation Program. After careful research and listening to cancer survivors, we determined that some cancer survivors, due to financial needs and other circumstances, were having difficulty getting to their appointments and treatments in McLennan County. Transportation should not be a roadblock to treatment for any cancer survivor. We prayed and asked God to help us establish a way to assist those cancer survivors needing transportation to their doctor appointments, chemotherapy, and radiation treatments. With the guidance of the Holy Spirit, we developed and adopted a policy that outlined assisting those recently diagnosed with cancer and those continuing their life journey with their transportation needs. Our board members and some of our members have driven our cancer clients to appointments in their private vehicles. I pray one day; God will bless us to have a van with insurance to fulfill this need.

Janice Ephraim is the Cancer Client Coordinator for Cattleya, and she determines their eligibility for us to gift them with the Waco Transit System bus passes. When we are not available to drive our clients or meet an abundance of calls, we provide them with a Waco Transit bus pass at no cost to the cancer survivor. Janice coordinates with McClinton Cancer Center and the Waco Transit Authority for the eligibility status of a potential client for the bus pass. We have a designated phone to receive calls from potential clients and word-of-mouth referrals. We also receive referrals from cancer centers and other nonprofit organizations. Cattleya has built relationships with cancer survivors and our communities through this program.

Cattleya Cancer Client Care Program (established in 2016)

Under the Cattleya Cancer Client Care Program, we visit cancer clients in the hospital, pray with them and their families before and during surgery, and give care baskets of essentials to the hospitals and cancer clients. We let them know that they are not alone. We also bring them reading materials and small gift bags to uplift their spirits. Occasionally, we have sat with a client in their home to relieve their caregiver. Giving care and support to cancer survivors can be challenging. Sometimes a caregiver needs time to themselves to recharge, which helps them take better care of the cancer survivor. We have comforted families of those cancer survivors who have reached the end of their life journey and have transitioned to a new life without pain.

The Baylor Scott and White McLane Children's Hospital

The Baylor Scott and White McLane Children's Hospital is a place where children with cancer receive the kind of care needed to fight for their lives. The compassionate and specialty care staff treat patients from the smallest preemies to young adults. In 2017, Cattleya first visited the McLane Cancer Care Unit. We provided books, toys, gloves and socks, blankets, and gift cards for them and their parents to help with essential needs. We watched as these brave and innocent young children came into the room set up for us with encouragement for all of us. We came to encourage them but received encouragement from them. They smiled and had hope for their future. Their faces showed determination as they pulled their oxygen tanks and medical apparatus alongside them. They walked with strength and purpose. Because of the treatment and medicine, cancer patients often feel cold, so blankets, socks, and gloves were to comfort them during that time.

As we interacted with the staff, parents, and children, God softly whispered, "this is your mission and service." Cattleya has adopted the cancer unit, and Toria and Lisa coordinate efforts throughout the year to visit and share the love with the children. I thank them for this great work in service to our babies. Thank you, God, for the opportunity to share your abundant love and gifts with McLane Children's Hospital.

Baylor Scott & White McClane Children's Camp Dreamcatcher

Upon our first visit, I realized McLane Children's Hospital sponsored a camp called Baylor Scott and White McLane's Children's Camp Dreamcatcher. Jenny

Damron is the coordinator of the camp. It is located in Burton, Texas, equipped with two lakes, cabins, lodges, and cabin counselors. There is also a full medical staff and medical center, which serves over one hundred young cancer survivor children and their siblings. The camp allows children to enjoy a "normal" week of fun designed just for them while still receiving treatment and care. We thank God for allowing us to continue to serve these kids and young people on their life journeys. We are inspired by their courage to fight for life. We continue to donate to this effort each year.

Susan G. Komen Foundation

According to Susan G. Komen's website, Komen.org, every 12 minutes a woman in the United States dies of breast cancer! One in eight women will be diagnosed with breast cancer in her lifetime. It is estimated that Komen has funded billions of dollars support breast cancer initiatives, and its mission is to save lives by meeting the most critical needs in our communities and investing in breakthrough research to prevent and cure breast cancer.

I have partnered with Susan G. Komen to fight the spread of breast cancer in our neighborhoods and families forever since 1990. Once Cattleya was established, we joined the fight as one of Komen's community volunteers and partners. I have served as an advocate for breast cancer survivors with Komen on its committees, board, race and walk for the cure because I wanted to make a difference in the lives of cancer survivors. My part was small but intentional. Komen has made an impact not only in the United States but in the world. Komen believes in the power of one, unifying to fight this disease together.

Through research, care, community, and action, Komen has touched the lives of many cancer survivors. They have assisted women in need of mammograms, in education, advocated for high-quality patient care, and in some cases financial needs. My most memorable experiences with Komen are the races and walks. These are yearly fundraisers, but more than that, it is how we (cancer survivors) build our relationships and encourages us to bond with neighbors, friends, families, and loved ones. It is seeing them year after year and knowing they are still in the fight for life and wholeness. It is being a part of the Komen phone banks and talking to cancer survivors who share their faith walk and living a life full of hope. As I have said before, God prepares us for our purpose and His plan before the mission call. Thank You, Lord, for the mission call of Komen.

Cattleya Whispers of Hope Rainbow Tea

In April 2018, we held our first Cattleya Whispers of Hope Rainbow Tea event. The purpose of the Cattleya Rainbow Tea was to share with our community the plight of cancer survivors, their courage, and God's grace. Faith is what continues to strengthen cancer survivors and leads us to victory through Christ.

We had seven tables (the number of completion and perfection in the Word of God) displayed in elegance and beauty. Our membership worked together in teams, and each team represented a cancer in memory of a loved one or our own cancer journey. The tables were displayed in a way that would bring hope and compassion through Jesus Christ to those cancer survivors who attended and an opportunity to share our stories with the community. There are many colors in a rainbow. Rainbows are a reminder of life and a covenant with God and man. Cancer has a rainbow of colors, and each color represents a particular cancer. The colors are a remembrance of life for all who may witness God's grace and hope. Thus, the name Cattleya Whispers of Hope Rainbow Tea.

What an awesome experience we shared that day. Our guests filled the room in the facility, and the Holy Spirit filled the atmosphere with His presence. God at work! Our speaker was Pastor Ruby Minnit, a woman of grace and love for God. Her topic was, "Our Condition Is Not Our Conclusion." The scripture reading was "We walk by faith and not by sight" 2 Corinthians 5:7. She spoke a powerful testimony and message about her cancer journey and trusting God for her recovery. She is a bilateral breast cancer survivor. We have now adopted this fundraising event annually.

Cattleya Fashion Show

In October 2019, we held our first Cattleya Fashion show. The purpose of the Cattleya Fashion Show was to allow all that attended to witness the beauty of cancer survivors. We want the world to see us as conquerors and not as victims! We live our lives without cancer or in remission because of God's grace. It is clearly not what is on the outside that counts, but what God has created in our hearts that will shine. Our lives bring new meaning to our purpose and for all to see and love Him.

Our speaker for the Cattleya Fashion Show was Gayle Culp, from Frisco, Texas. She is the former recording artist of the Gospel Truthettes of Malaco records. Gayle is a phenomenal woman with a heartfelt story of a mother's love for her child with a life-threatening medical condition. She talked about what happens when the insurance is limited, and a loved one needs help. What do you do? Where do you go? Who do you seek to fix the problem? She talked about these in her message. We were inspired and blessed by her testimony. We witnessed the miracle of God moving on behalf of a family struggling to survive. He opened doors and changed hearts to help this child with her recovery.

She shared with us what our cancer survivors face from the moment they receive their diagnosis until the last test is taken that states all results are clear. In the meantime, our faith remains rooted in God, our Healer! On that day, we celebrate and ring our bell! God also allowed my story about my cancer journey, the establishment of Cattleya, and the purpose of the Cattleya

Fashion Show to be featured in the Anchor Newspaper, our local newspaper, during the planning of the Fashion Show. We appreciate all the help that Linda (Cattleya member) and J.L. Crawford have given to promote Cattleya and for giving cancer survivors a voice. They have been a blessing to us.

A big thank you to the initiative of Rachel Pate and the Centex African American Chamber of Commerce. I have been blessed to appear on KWTX Morning Show with Ann Harder to promote Cattleya, "A Celebration of Life" event, and to bring community interest to our cancer survivors and our foundation. You can do the same thing in your communities to bring awareness to cancer and the fight for a cure.

> *"I will praise You, for I am fearfully (beautifully) and wonderfully made; marvelous are Your works, and that my soul knows well..." How precious also are Your thoughts of me, O God. How great is the sum of them. If I should count them, they would be more in number than the sand; when I wake, I am still with You."*
>
> **~PSALM 139:14,17-18 NKJV**

May God continue to bless you!
Victorious!

Testimonies from Cattleya Clients:

<u>Mrs. Jacqueline Mitchell</u>

"My mother, Jacqueline Mitchell, a strong woman and cancer survivor, was diagnosed with Multiple Myeloma in 2015. I asked Cattleya to help my Mama on her journey. And they did! They visited, prayed, and brought her to her doctor appointments when I had to work. They helped us all the way to the end of her journey. I still received calls eight months after her homegoing. I know that I am remembered, supported, and loved by Cattleya." Brenda Johnson, daughter of Jacqueline Mitchell.

<u>Ms. Maria Skinner</u>
<u>Cancer survivor</u>
A text message from Ms. Skinner:
"Good afternoon,
Even in the midst of my storm, I see God working it out for me. I just want to say thanks to you and to Cattleya for helping me get to my doctor appointments caring, concern,

and support. I love you, Min. Henry, have a truly blessed day." Ms. Maria Skinner.

> AND JESUS CAME AND SPOKE TO THEM SAYING, "ALL AUTHORITY HAS BEEN GIVEN TO ME IN HEAVEN AND ON EARTH. GO THEREFORE AND MAKE DISCIPLES OF ALL THE NATIONS, BAPTIZING THEM IN THE NAME OF THE FATHER AND THE SON AND OF THE HOLY SPIRIT, TEACHING THEM TO OBSERVE ALL THINGS THAT I HAVE COMMANDED YOU; AND LO, I AM WITH YOU ALWAYS, EVEN TO THE END OF THE AGE." AMEN.

MATTHEW 28:16-30 NKJV

CHAPTER 14:

MY LORD AND SAVIOR

———— ༄୨୨୧ ————

Transformation (The Church, The Great Commission and Me)

he mission of the church is to glorify God, spread the Gospel of Jesus Christ to the lost, and make Christ-like disciples out of those who follow, fellowship with one another, and seek Him in prayer. Through the direction of the Holy Spirit, the church mentorship, communion, mission, preaching, teaching, and discipleship spreads the seed of the gospel to the world. The church is her people, and each person is created to please God. We were created to worship Him and to do His Will.

My Love for God and the Church

> "*A new command I give to you, that you love one another; as I have loved you, that you also love one another. By this all will know that you are My disciples, if you have love for one another.*"
>
> ~JOHN 13:34-35 NKJV

As I have said before, I did not grow up in the church, but I had a yearning desire to learn about God and discover him for myself. I believe God was continuously watching over me and keeping me close to Him. I had to go through the process of pain and the seasons of trials in life to know how much God genuinely loves me. He is constantly working in my life to fulfill His plan and purpose for me.

He is the Father, and I am the child. With His blood, Jesus saved me from myself and hell. Thank You, Lord, for Your faithfulness. I am grateful that my mind and spirit cannot focus without You in my life every day. My love for You compels me. I always desire to speak to You when I awake in the morning and throughout the day. My worship radiates from You, Jesus, our Lord, and Savior. You shed Your innocent blood for me who is guilty so that I would not have to pay the price for my sinful mind and heart (John 15:13-17 NKJV). Your presence in my life is welcomed.

As the songwriter Jonathan McReynolds so eloquently wrote, "I will move whatever agenda I need to so You can feel welcomed to come in and live in me." God, I am willing to lay at Your feet, my Lord, and give all of myself to You! Yes, Lord. You have done so much for me. When I wake afraid in the night, Your love protects and strengthens me. When I am lonely, You hold me close and tenderly soothe me. No one else knows my pain as You do. No one else knows my sorrow like You know it. You, my God, are the Spirit that is all-knowing. You are everywhere and have all power. No one else can comfort and give me peace like You. I am grateful for the continuous relationship we have bonded together in love and faith. I love to be near You and to hear You speak to me. My heart leaps with gladness in your presence, and I worship You.

> *"Rejoice always, pray without ceasing, in everything give thanks; for this is the Will of God in Christ Jesus for you."*
>
> ~1 THESSALONIANS 5: 16-18 NKJV

Pleasant Olive Missionary Baptist Church and Ecclesia – The People

> *"And I also say to you that you are Peter, and on this rock, I will build My church, and the gates of Hades shall not prevail against it."*
>
> ~MATTHEW 16:18 NKJV

Pleasant Olive Missionary Baptist Church is the first church that the Holy Spirit led me to serve under the servant leadership of Pastor Monty E. Francis. I was invited to attend for the first time by my dear sister, Rosetta Thompson. Rosetta and I met at the Department of Veteran Affairs (VA) Regional Office in Waco, Texas, where we both worked. She was well known and respected in the VA, the church, and the community. Rosetta had a servant's heart and walked with humility. It was clear that she loved the Lord. She was elegant and beautiful on both the inside and out. I had been searching for a church for several months before the Holy Spirit led me to Pleasant Olive. My grandmother and mother planted the seed, Rosetta watered the seed, and now God was about to give the increase in my life.

The first time I heard Pastor Francis preach the Word of God, I was in awe of God. I knew I had to hear more. I hungered and thirsted for more of God every day. So, I continued to attend. I was also looking for a church with children's programs to enhance Devlin's spiritual, physical, and mental growth. I asked the Holy Spirit for a special place where my family could grow closer to God.

Have you ever sought that kind of Bible-based nurturing for your family? If you are looking for a church home, look for a church with a sound biblical doctrine that will welcome your involvement and use your spiritual gifts. Ask the Holy Spirit to reveal to you what your spiritual gifts are. Seek a church that will encourage your worship and not just entertain you. Keep in mind this is not a membership but a doctrine of love, fellowship, and devotion to God.

One day I was sitting in church eagerly and intensely listening to the Word of God. Then, something came over me like a burning fire, and I had no choice but to surrender and welcome God into my life. Do you remember your conversion and transformation experience? What was your Damascus Road (ACTS 9:1-19) journey like? Has salvation happened to you in a similar way? What is your testimony?

At that moment, I let go of my way and experienced the love, blessings, and compassion of my God. It is an indescribable feeling of joy and heaven. I was saved by grace! This was God's ultimate plan and gift for my life. His plan was for me to know Him and to build a lasting relationship with Him. Everything I had experienced led up to this moment. This was all part of His plan for my destiny and His glory! It is about the love of salvation through Jesus Christ and the gift of grace He wants to give to each of us. I now must share His love with the world.

My husband Joseph did not come right away, but I kept praying for him. My prayers were finally answered, and God touched his heart and took our family to another level together. Since that day, our lives have continuously been blessed. We continue to pray for each of our family members to answer their call, but in the meantime, we serve the Lord wholeheartedly. We continue to serve and glorify Him today. The road is not always easy but so much richer in heavenly treasures.

God birthed a spiritual bond between Rosetta Thompson and me that continued until her death. I can still remember in my heart our treasured memories of love and growth with conversations orchestrated by God. I miss her dearly and think of her often as I do my Mama. She became my mentor, teacher, dear friend, and prayer partner. Prayer became an intricate part of my daily life and still is today. The discipleship training I received at Pleasant Olive changed my entire life forever. Rosetta and I were so close that she accepted our request to become Devlin's Godmother.

I truly admired and loved her. She was missionary-minded and shared that love and compassion with me. She lived the life of a woman of God outlined in the scripture of Titus 2. She was a faithful servant who pioneered the way for many Christian women through Christ. She had four grown boys of her own, who were close, but Rosetta had many children. I am so grateful and humbled to feel like I am among them.

Who is your Rosetta Thompson? Has God placed someone in your life that assures you of God's love for you? Someone who implores you to seek Him daily. Has God blessed your life and shared with you a journey of missional living? A journey filled with a deepened understanding of God's character and His mission. What is it that motivates you? I am motivated by the desire to please God.

I am an Ambassador for Christ, a Kingdom citizen, living to spread the Good News and the Gospel of Jesus Christ (His life, death, and Resurrection) to my neighbors, family, friends, and all who will listen. Lord, help me to be bold for You! Even though the journey is not always easy, and I stumble on occasion, I know God can pick me up, dust me off, and put me back on the path He has set for me. He can do the same for you. If you have experienced this journey, you already know what I mean.

I would be remiss if I did not share my endearing friendship with two extraordinary men of God. They both followed the teachings of Jesus, loved their families, humbled themselves in service to Him, and were instrumental in my growth and development as a minister.

Dr. Willie E. Clarke Sr., Pastor of Pleasant Olive Missionary Baptist Church and Assistant Pastor, Rev. Dr. Everett James.

Pastor Clarke answered God's call to shepherd our church when we needed an abundance of love and healing. We all loved to hear our beloved Pastor bellow out one of those spiritual songs, which penetrated our hearts deeply, before his electrifying sermons. The one I loved to hear him sing was "I Won't Complain." Dr. Clarke, through the word, brought into our church the concept of "fran-gelism." Evangelize your neighbors, family members, and friends through the word of God. He would say, *"Go home to thy friends and tell them how great things the Lord hath done for thee, and hath had compassion on thee."* (Mark 5:19 KJV)

I remember him once calling our congregation together for a washing of the feet ceremony. He washed the feet of every member who attended and demonstrated the humility of Christ's humble example of love (John

13:1-20 NKJV). Christ washed His disciples' feet during the Last Supper to demonstrate humility and the meaning of a servant leader. Pastor Clarke wanted us to lead as Christ taught us to do without judgement or condemnation but with love.

Pastor Clarke was instrumental in guiding me through faith to become an effective minister in service to Christ. He knew how important education was to me and encouraged me to enter the seminary. I will always be grateful to him for his leadership and his friendship. "Henry, you got to learn how to work smarter, not harder." A piece of advice he dropped on me when I was overwhelmed. Sometimes I did not understand the decision-making process, but I am thankful I was obedient and followed him.

Pastor Clarke and his wife, Miss Robbie, went home to glory while serving in Pleasant Olive. Losing our Pastor and First Lady was like losing a family member. I felt the pain, as we all did, all over again of losing a dear loved one. It was as if someone had stabbed me with a knife right into my heart. I choose to honor his memory and legacy by remembering his devotion to Christ's teachings, love, and forgiveness. To this day, I can hear him speaking words of wisdom to me and gently guiding me with kindness and telling those jokes that kept me smiling. He is sorely missed by many and certainly by the Henry family. Pastor Francis, Pastor Clarke, and Rev. Dr. James all loved the Word of God and demonstrated great love for His people.

Dr. J., as we so lovingly referred to him, became Interim Pastor after Pastor Francis moved to Dallas, Texas, and again when Pastor Clarke went home to glory. Dr. J and Pat James, his wife, became our loving friends and still have a special place in our hearts today. For years, Pat and I celebrated our birthdays together. Dr. J. is a visionary and a humble man of God. When I approached him with the news that God had called me into the ministry as a minister, he began to pray for me, mentor my ministry development, and share the profound spiritual aspects of this ministerial calling.

Dr. J. gave me a book, "The New Minister's Manual," by Dr. Paul W. Powell, former Dean of the George R. Truett Theological Seminary at Baylor University in Waco, Texas. This book's purpose is to encourage and guide new ministers seeking to learn how to conduct the duties and responsibilities of a preacher. It is a seed planted in new ministers and inspires us to seek God for growth and development. God continues to give the increase to those He has chosen for this work. Dr. J., through the movement of the Holy Spirit, was instrumental in building up the Education and Mission Ministries of Pleasant Olive and appointed me as director for both. As an upcoming minister, this was a great challenge and a welcomed opportunity to serve.

Through the Holy Spirit, I was compelled to seek the Word of God for wisdom and reach out to Christians who were experienced in church education and mission work at the Waco Regional Baptist Association in Waco, Texas, and in Pleasant Olive. Together, we served the community in many ways, from door-to-door evangelism to volunteering in the local schools, a Neighborhood Block Party, and more. Pastor Frances appointed me as Youth director many years ago. I continued to work with our children, teachers, and parents alongside Rev. Robert Cummings after he accepted the calling as our Youth Pastor. With the guidance of the Holy Spirit, the leadership of our shepherds, and a loving staff of Christian men and women, we were able to bring to our church programs geared toward the spiritual and mental development of all our children and young people.

All of what I do is to glorify God and to edify His Kingdom. I am grateful to Pleasant Olive, Pastor Francis, Pastor Clarke, and Dr. J. for allowing me the opportunity to serve and the space to be stretched by God for His service. Thank You, Lord, for the gift of grace.

> *"And Jesus answered him, the first of all commandments is, Hear, O Israel; The Lord our God is one Lord; and thou shall love the Lord thy God with all thy heart, and with all thy soul, and with all thy mind, and with all thy strength: This is the first commandment. And the second is like, namely this, thou shall love thy neighbor as thyself; There is none other commandment greater than these."*
>
> ~MARK 12:29-31 KJV

Love thy neighbor!

A Compassionate God - An Encouraging Journey

> *In the beginning was the Word, and the Word*
> *was with God, and the Word was God. He was*
> *in the beginning with God. All things were made*
> *through him, and without him was not anything*
> *made that was made.*
>
> ~JOHN 1:1-3 NKJV

I have the "Living Life" framed poem hanging in my study room, so I can remember the gift of life and encourage my spirit to dream because God is the giver of dreams. The moment I saw it hanging in the store, I was drawn to purchase it. It breathes the importance of life in a simple way. We can all understand and appreciate the gift of life when we realize how precious each moment truly is to us.

At a point in my life, I prayed to God to help me in my battle with weight loss. In my life after cancer, this was a space where I was struggling. As a cancer survivor, I knew I had to work to combat this area to continue to fight for life. I cannot say that weight gain caused or even contributed to cancer growing in me, but I can say being overweight was certainly not good for me in any way. While society has judged obesity shamefully and harshly, God is compassionate. It is a disease like alcohol, drug addiction, or mental illness. It is a fight within yourself! Sometimes it feels like trying to climb Mt. Everest or breaking free of a giant cobweb. God had a plan for me, and all I had to do was ask Him to help me. If you have ever tried to lose weight or struggle to maintain a healthy lifestyle, you understand what I mean. "I can do all things through Christ Who gives me strength." (Philippians 4:13 NIV)

In February 2018, I went through a rigid body overhaul and lost forty pounds. I exercised and changed my way of thinking about food and me. I felt great again! My breathing was no longer shallow, and my energy level increased tremendously. I could wear fitted clothing again instead of wearing oversized tops to cover my shame. I was no longer embarrassed by the way I looked. My confidence increased so much, and I walked with purpose. Some thin people, like I once was, have no idea the pain overweight people suffer and the sneering remarks from some cut deep.

And, by the way, they do not help anyone. As a child and even as an adult, I was always fit. I was always in the single digits in clothing and never had to try on anything. I am sure some of you know exactly what I mean and have your own personal testimonies. But, when I became much older, my body began to change, and I started to add on the weight. I was about in my middle fifties.

I attribute it to stress, taking care of others, and neglecting my health and wellness. As women, we tend to do that often, and I am no different. We must keep in mind when we age, our bodies change, and we must be mindful of the changes. "For all have sinned and fall short of the glory of God."

But God can offer us a way full of grace and love toward ourselves through forgiveness.

I must thank Devlin for encouraging me forward in this continuous fight for a healthy lifestyle in such a loving way. I thank God for giving me ears to hear and a heart to accept change. I am blessed to have recognized my brokenness and the will to seek Him for healing. God chooses each one of us for His work, and He chose Devlin to carry forth His message of strength and determination to me.

As a Christmas present in 2017, Devlin purchased a set of Beats earphones for me and encouraged me to join the gym. I did!! I was now on the road to weight loss recovery. But wait! I had to look at myself and do some self-cleansing. I had to be willing to change old habits and forgive myself. I really wanted to live a meaningful life, and I am thankful to God that I did not have a stroke, heart attack, or become a diabetic. God gave me another chance to live a life full of hope with great expectations for the future. Our Father is like that, you know. I made it through cancer and will continue on my life journey with new expectations and desires. I continue to walk in faith, knowing God is forever present in my life. More than that, I remain anchored in the Lord, and He remains steadfast in my life.

"My Soul Has Been Anchored in The Lord" Original Lyrics by Douglas Miller

"Though the storms keep on raging in my life, and sometimes it's hard to tell my night from day, still that hope that lies within is reassured, as I keep my eyes upon the distant shore; I know He'll lead me safely to that blessed place He has prepared. But if the storms don't cease, and if the wind keeps on blowing, my soul has been anchored in the Lord."

My Father is constantly fighting for me, and my life journey continues through Him. I live to bear witness to His glory another day.

God's Amazing Grace

"

TO WHOM MUCH IS GIVEN, MUCH IS REQUIRED.

———

LUKE 12:48 ESV

CHAPTER 15:

THE ASSURANCE OF GOD

―――――――――∽ᑭᑫᑲ―――――――――

> *"May the Lord answer you in the day of trouble;*
>
> *May the Name of the God of Jacob defend you;*
>
> *May He send you help from the sanctuary, and strengthen you out of Zion;*
>
> *May He remember all your offerings and accept your burnt sacrifice.*
>
> *May He grant you according to your heart's desire and fulfill all your purpose.*
>
> *We will rejoice in your salvation,*

and in the Name of our God, we will set up our banners!

May the Lord fulfill all your petitions.

Now I know that the Lord saves His anointed; He will answer him from

His Holy Heaven with the saving strength of His right hand.

Some trust in chariots, and some in horses; but we will remember the Name of the Lord our God.

They have bowed down and fallen; but we have risen and stand upright.

Save, Lord!

May the King answer us when we call.

~PSALM 20 NKJV

As we come to the close of this writing, I am thankful to God for walking with me and reassuring me that I have something to share with you. I will admit at times, my thoughts were for me to walk away, but God kept whispering that this was necessary for me and beneficial to others. I was not doing this just for me but for the cancer survivor recently diagnosed, for the family member who does not understand or know what to do but is a co-cancer survivor in this battle. This was also written for the child who wants to help their parent to be happy and well.

How do we cope with life after cancer? We kiss our children and watch them grow. We praise God for the abundance of life and love. We remain steadfast and willing to serve others in ministry. We live our lives each day with gratitude. We realize we are our brother's keeper and encourage those who are distraught that they, too, can stand up and be strong in Christ Jesus.

I had to share some intimate parts of my life, showing how to dance in the rain. I pray you realize that through Christ, you too can accomplish great things. You can humbly serve your communities, build lasting relationships, and trust God in the process. He holds the answer to your questions and your mission call.

This book is written to plant seeds of hope in you and to encourage you to live your life with joy. I want you to get up in the morning ready to face your challenges and to fight another day with victory and love in Christ Jesus. The Holy Word is our instructions and our way to defeat the enemy. It is filled with the tools we need to accomplish every life goal on our journey. The Holy Word teaches us how to overcome fear and exercise our Kingdom authority.

Thank you for the opportunity to share my story with you, and I hope it will make a difference in your life. May God bless you and keep you always.

In His Service and Your Friendship,

SPIRITUAL REFLECTIONS FROM WITHIN THE HEART

In Scriptures, Hymns, And Poetry

A Love Letter To GOD

I humble myself before You, Lord, and I thank You for the opportunity You have given me to serve You. I am so grateful that You continue to take the time to keep growing, developing, cleansing, and preparing me for Your purpose with unconditional love. The same love I am required by You to give to others.

If I may be honest, I know sometimes I was not always listening clearly to Your voice, but You remained patient with me. I have learned in our relationship to trust You even if what You are telling me to do makes no sense to my natural mind. I am willing to take the risk. I am blessed and thankful that You allow me to become intimate with You. I open the door to my heart and continuously yearn for a deeper relationship with You, Father. You are the one who has been there when the road was rough and uncertain. I found and continue to find peace in You.

We have walked together for a long time, and looking back, and I am blessed to have You on the path with me. You have constantly been my guiding light, and I have no reason to feel alone or fearful. I do not have to feel a distaste for isolation. Who else would sacrifice His only Son just for me? Jesus is loving, faithful, and merciful. He leads with humility and compassion. How can I not work at being like Him?

I love our quiet times together and our precious walks in the garden of life, where my Lord and Savior, Jesus Christ, reveals the truth to me. I find myself fighting the temptation to rise up in anger when I see wrongs being done in this world and even sometimes to me. Forgiveness is so important, and I continue to learn this kind of love through the teachings of Jesus Christ. I continue to feel compassion and love because of You toward others. My hands and my heart continue to remain open in serving You.

Because of Your Grace, I desire to search my heart and remove those barriers that keep me away from You and replace them with love and humility. I yearn to mirror Your leadership on my life journey and share it with others. It is Your strength that is Perfect and strengthens me when I am in the face of adversity and trials.

You encouraged me and inspired me to step out of my comfort zone, depend on You, and through faith, work with others to establish Cattleya Foundation of Hope as a nonprofit Christian cancer foundation in McLennan County. All honor and glory belong to You. It is through You I do not fear the unknown or the opposition and disapproval of others because, above all, I must follow You and be ready to go forward when You say GO!

I trust You, and I am confident that I can depend on You in any situation, calamity, or challenge that may come my way. You continue to remind me that I am a part of Your purpose and plan. It seems like it took a lifetime for me to realize how important I am to You. I believe You and have no reason to doubt Your sincerity because I know firsthand what You have done and can do in my life. Trusting You is my assurance You will keep Your promises. It is why my obedience to You is crucial in my life. Simply,

I love You, Lord, and will obey You. Forgive me for losing focus at times and thank You for guiding me. I continue to reverence You, my God, with my heart. Your will, not my will!

With love, Your daughter,

Sandra

A grateful child

Your Will, Your Way, with Your Word

> "The Lord is my Shepherd, I shall not want."
>
> ~PSALM 23:1 NKJV

Love

And so, we know and rely on the love God has for us. God is love. Whoever lives in love lives in God, and God in them.

~1 JOHN 4:16 NIV

Whoever says he is in the Light and hates his brother is still in the darkness until now. Whoever loves his brother abides in the Light, and in him there is no cause for stumbling in him.

~1 JOHN 2:9-10

Have mercy on me, O God, according to your steadfast love; according to your abundant mercy blot out my transgressions. Wash me thoroughly from my iniquity, and cleanse me from my sin.

~PSALM 51:1-2

He must become increase, but I must decrease.

~JOHN 3:30

I love You, O Lord, my strength. The Lord is my rock and my fortress and my deliverer, my God, my rock, in whom I take refuge, my shield, and the horn of my salvation, my stronghold. I call upon the Lord, who is worthy to be praised, and I am saved from my enemies.

~PSALM 18:1-3

…if we are faithless, he remains faithful—for he cannot deny himself.

~2 TIMOTHY 2:13

Family and Friends

> We then that are strong ought to (are obligated) to bear the infirmities of the weak and not to please ourselves.
>
> ~ROMANS 15:1

> He replied to him, "Who is my mother, and who are my brothers?" Pointing to His disciples, He said, "Here are my mother and my brothers. For whoever does the Will of my Father in heaven is my brother and my sister and mother."
>
> ~MATTHEW 12:48-50

> Do all things without complaining or disputing that you may become blameless and harmless children of God without fault in the midst of a crooked and perverse generation, among whom you shine as lights in the world, holding fast the word of life, so that I may rejoice in the day of Christ that I have not run in vain or labored in vain.
>
> ~PHILIPPIANS 2:14-16

Hope

Now the God of hope fill you with joy and peace in believing, that you may abound in hope, through the power of the Holy Spirit.

~ROMANS 15:13

Rejoicing in hope, patient in tribulation, continuing steadfastly in prayer.

~ROMANS 12:12

Rejoice always, pray without ceasing, in everything give thanks, for this is the will of God for your life in Christ Jesus.

~1 THESSALONIANS 5:16-18

Cast your burdens on the Lord, and He shall sustain you; He shall never permit the righteous to be moved.

~PSALM 55:22

Unity

And above all these put on love, which binds everything together in perfect harmony.

~COLOSSIANS 3:14

There is neither Jew or Greek, there is neither slave or free, there is no male and female, for you are all one in Christ Jesus.

~GALATIANS 3:28

I, therefore, the prisoner of the Lord,] beseech you to walk worthy of the calling with which you were called, with all lowliness and gentleness, with longsuffering, bearing with one another in love, endeavoring to keep the unity of the Spirit in the bond of peace. There is one body and one Spirit, just as you were called in one hope of your calling; one Lord, one faith, one baptism; one God and Father of all, who is above all, and through all, and in you all.

~EPHESIANS 4:1-6

Togetherness

Rejoice in the Lord, always. Again, I will say, rejoice.

~PHILIPPIANS4:4

Finally, brethren, whatever things are true, whatever things are noble, whatever things are just, whatever things are pure, whatever things are lovely, whatever things are of good report, if there is any virtue and if anything is praiseworthy, meditate on these things.

~PHILIPPIANS4:8

For as we have many members in one body, but all the members do not have the same function, so we, being many, are one body in Christ, and individually members of one another.

~ROMANS 12:4-5

Arise, shine, for your light has come, and the glory of the Lord rises upon you.

~ISAIAH 60:1

Worry

Turn your worries over to the Lord. He will keep you going. He will never let godly people be shaken.

~PSALM 55:22

Who of you by worrying can add a single hour to your life?

~LUKE 12:25

Worry weighs a person down; an encouraging word cheers a person up.

~PROVERBS 12:25

FORGIVENESS

> *He is so rich in kindness and grace that He purchased our freedom with the blood of His Son and forgave our sins.*
>
> ~EPHESIANS 1:17

> *Get rid of all bitterness, rage, and anger, brawling and slander, along with every form of malice. Be kind and compassionate to one another, forgiving each other, just as in Christ God forgave you.*
>
> ~EPHESIANS 4:31-32

HYMNALS

——— ⟋⟍⟋⟍ ———

SWING LOW, SWEET CHARIOT
Wallace Willis, Lyricist
(Choctaw Freedman) 1820-1880

Swing low, sweet chariot,

Coming for to carry me home.

Swing low, sweet chariot,

Coming for to carry me home.

I looked over Jordan, and what did I see,

Coming for to carry me home.

A band of angels coming after me,

Coming for to carry me home. Oh,

If you get there before I do, coming for to carry me home,

Tell all my friends I'm coming too,

Coming for to carry me home. Oh,

The brightest day that ever I saw

Coming for to carry me home.

When Jesus washed my sins away,

Coming for to carry me home. Oh,

I'm sometimes up and sometimes down,

Coming for to carry me home.

But still my soul feels heav'nly bound,

Coming for to carry me home.

Source: One Lord, One Faith, One Baptism.

An African American Ecumenical Hymnal #611

Blessed Assurance
Frances Jane Crosby
Phoebe Palmer Knapp

Written in 1873

Blessed Assurance Jesus is Mine!

Oh, what a foretaste of glory divine!

Heir of salvation, purchased by God,

Born of His Spirit, washed in His blood.

Chorus:

This is my story, this is my song,

Praising my Savior all the day long;

This is my story, this is my song,

Praising my Savior all the day long.

Perfect submission, perfect delight,

Vision of rapture now burst on my sight;

Angels, descending, bring from above

Echoes of mercy, whispers of love.

Perfect submission, all is at rest

I in my Savior am happy and blest,

Watching and waiting, looking above,

Filled with His goodness, lost in His love.

I Surrender All
Justin W. Van DeVenter
Winfield S. Weeden
Published 1896

All to Jesus, I surrender

All to Him I freely give;

I will ever love and trust Him,

In His presence daily live.

I surrender all, I surrender all,

All to Thee, my blessed Savior,

I surrender all.

Victory Is Mine
Written in 1991
By Dorothy Norwood and Alvin Darling
Lyricist – Dorothy Norwood

Victory is mine,
Victory is mine,
Victory today is mine.

I told Satan to get thee behind,
Victory today is mine.

Victory is mine,
Victory is mine,
Victory today is mine.

I told Satan to get thee behind,
Victory today is mine.

Joy is mine,
Joy is mine,
I know that joy is mine.

I told Satan to get thee behind,
I know that joy is mine.

Happiness is mine,
Happiness is mine,
Happiness today is mine.

I told Satan to get thee behind,
Happiness today is mine.

When I rose this morning,
I didn't have no doubt,
I knew that the Lord would bring me out.

I fell on my knees,
Said, "Lord help me please"
Got up singing and shouting the victory.

Victory is mine,
Victory is mine,
Victory today is mine.

I told Satan to get thee behind,
Victory today is mine

Victory is mine,
Victory is mine,
Victory today is mine.

I told Satan
I told Satan
I told Satan
To get thee behind,
Victory today is mine

PURPOSE
By Roy Lessin

Purpose to seek Him –

He will always be your reward.

Purpose to follow Him –

He will always lead the way.

Purpose to enjoy Him –

He will always be your dearest friend.

Purpose to praise Him –

He will always be the Worthy One.

Purpose to trust Him –

He will always be your faithful Provider.

Purpose to please Him –

He will always give you what is good.

Purpose to be totally His –

He will always be totally yours!

Living Life Poem
by Bonnie L. Mohr

"Life is not a race but indeed a journey. Be honest. Work hard. Be choosy. Say "thank you", "I love you", and "great job" to someone each day. Go to church, take time for prayer. The Lord giveth and the Lord taketh. Let your handshake mean more than pen and paper. Love your life and what you have been given, it is not accidental – search for your purpose and do it as best you can. Dreaming does matter. It allows you to become that which you aspire to be. Laugh often. Appreciate the little things in life and enjoy them. Some of the best things really are free. Do not worry, less wrinkles are more becoming. Forgive, it frees the soul. Take time for yourself – plan for longevity. Recognize the special people you've been blessed to know. Live for today, enjoy the moment.

ACKNOWLEDGEMENTS

—⁓ꙮꙮ⁓—

Cattleya Godly Speakers

2015 Sis Hattie Mae Black – Downsville Baptist Church

(A Celebration of Life Luncheon, Spa at Canyon Oaks)

2016 Cindy Janecka – International Motivational Speaker and Author

(Breast Cancer Survivor)

2016-Present Rev. Dr. Edward L. Ross, Sr. Pastor Abundant Love Fellowship Church

(Invocation)

(Sister cancer journey ended)

2017 Connie Hall-Baylor Law Professor

(Metastatic Breast Cancer Survivor)

2018 Rev. Pastor Joe Bedford, Sr. Pastor
Living Hope Missionary Baptist Church
(Cancer Survivor)

2018 Rochonda Neal – Baylor University
(Kidney Transplant Recipient)

2019 Rev. Pastor Ruby Minnit, Sr. Pastor
Greater Love Church
(Breast Cancer Survivor)

2019 Gayla Culp – Recording Artist, Frisco, Texas
(Child Medical Condition)

Thank you for your willingness to serve.

2021 CATTLEYA BOARD AND MEMBERSHIP

CATTLEYA BOARD AND FOUNDING MEMBERS

- Rev. Dr. Sandra Henry, CEO/President
- Shelia Ross, Executive Director
- Toria Smith-Loughridge, Finance Officer
- Lisa Ware, New Membership
- Sandra Montgomery resigned due to illness

CATTLEYA MEMBERSHIP

- Linda Crawford, Recording Secretary, and newest Board Member
- Keisha Bridges-Miller, Communication and Media
- Pastor Ruby Minnit, Chaplain
- Min. Rosie Douglas, Membership Birthday Coordinator
- Janice Ephraim, Cancer Client Coordinator
- Keisha Bridges-Miller, Communication and MediaPastor Ruby Minnit, Chaplain
- Teresa Courtney

- Ulanda Crawford
- Beverly Donahue
- Brenda Johnson
- Gloria Mann
- Maggie Majors
- Sandra Maxwell
- Gwendolyn Ryan
- Gloria Thomas
- Annie Turner
- Quience Wright

We have planted the seed of hope into one another and joined Cattleya in this fight against all cancers, but Jesus Christ through His power and wisdom determines the increase and growth of Cattleya. He chose us for this mission, and this is what happens when women say yes to God. Thank You, Lord, for Your pursuit of each of us. Our lives have been changed forever and we are blessed. We may not always agree but we rely on You to guide us and show us the way.

With sisterly love and respect for one another!

There are so many of you who inspired me and actually provided your time, gifts, talents, and love during the birthing of this writing. You prayed for me and encouraged me to keep going and not to give up. If I were to include everyone, it would fill this entire book and almost did! You all know who you are and my love for you will never fade. You are all extraordinary people of God. Thank you!

Throughout my cancer journey and while I remained obedient in the building of Cattleya, my missional journey after cancer, these were some of the shoulders I had to lean on and arms that had to hold me up. Thank you with all my heart!

➤ LaVeda Brown, Retired and Rachel Pate

➤ Centex African American Chamber of Commerce

➤ Thank you, both, for your help in getting Cattleya recognized in the community.

➤ The Madison Cooper House Foundation and the Waco Foundation

➤ Thank you for your continuous support and educational nonprofit training.

- Kakes by Kate, Rev. Larry and Min. Valencia Parks Catering, Valerie Willis

- Thank you for sharing with me your culinary gifts and stretching out your hand to help in my times of need.

- Matthew Polk, Executive Director, and Alexis Christensen, Community Engagement

- Prosper Waco

- Thank you, Matthew and Alexis, for being friends and consistent supporters of Cattleya. Thank you, Matthew, for conducting our Cattleya Board training session. Thank you both for lending a listening ear when I was unsure what to do next.

- First Baptist Woodway, Dr. Paul Sands, Sr. Pastor

- Carver Park Baptist Church, Dr. Gaylon Foreman, Sr. Pastor, cancer survivor and author

- Thank you, Pastor Sands and Pastor Foreman, for opening your church doors and allowing us the space to witness the move of God at our first Cattleya Rainbow Tea and first Cattleya Fashion

Show. May God continue to bless you and keep you in His Perfect peace.

- Byron Wilkerson, Thank you for all of your help with The Cattleya Fashion Show
- Marilyn Banks, Marilyn Gift Shop
- Thank you, Marilyn, for being a beacon of light to so many Christian sisters and brothers who need someone to stand up for justice and speak for them. You are a Christian leader that we welcome in our humble service to God. Thank you for your help during the Cattleya Fashion Show and presenting your models and fashion.
- Keisha Bridges-Miller, Prosperity Tax, Inc.
- Ke'sha Lopez, KWTX and Jasmin Caldwell, KCEN
- Jennifer Jefferson
- Thank you for always being there when I needed encouragement and prayer. Thank you for the laughter and sharing a cup of hot tea.
- Eval Montgomery

➢ Thank you for encouraging me not to give up in the face of adversity.

➢ Janice Matthews, owner and mortician of Doris Miller Memorial Park Cemetery

➢ Thank you, Janice, for your continuous support through my battle with cancer

➢ Commissioner Lester L. Gibson and Mrs. Coque Gibson

➢ Thank you for the many years of wisdom and encouraging words gave to me and having my back in tough situations. Thank you for promoting, introducing, and allowing Cattleya the airtime at the Hip Hop Radio Station, 94.5 FM ("If We Only Knew, What We Could Do!") when we needed the publicity.

ABOUT SANDRA HENRY

My earthly birth name which was given by my mama is Sandra, but my Heavenly Father knows me as His Daughter in Christ. I am blessed that God has welcomed me into His Kingdom Family. I am grateful that He calls me beloved DAUGHTER!

Dr. Sandra Henry is an ordained minister of the Abundant Love Fellowship Church under the leadership of Dr. Edward L. Ross, Sr. Pastor. Dr. Henry has served in ministry for over thirty years in the areas of Sunday School, Youth, Education Ministry, Mission Ministry, and Women's Ministry. Dr. Henry's passion has been to humbly serve the youth and young adults in our communities and recently, to serve cancer survivors.

Dr. Henry holds a doctoral degree in Theology with honors from the American International Bible Institute and Seminary. She gives recognition and is grateful to

Dr. Dean Palmer, Baylor University professor and pastor for over fifty years, for encouraging and inspiring her to become a writer. Dr. Henry attended Northwestern State University in Natchitoches, Louisiana.

Dr. Henry served in the United States Army, and she is an honorably discharged veteran. She was born and raised on the East coast. She hails from New York City (Manhattan), New York, and her husband grew up in Washington D.C. but was born in Philadelphia, Pennsylvania. Dr. Henry and her husband relocated to Waco, Texas, in 1986 with her family from Louisiana after Joseph retired from the military. Together they have four children, five grandchildren, and many great grandchildren.

Dr. Henry is active in the Central Texas community, and has worked with Stars Book Club at J. H. Hines Elementary school in East Waco, Texas and serves on their Advisory Board; Prosper Waco on their Community Engagement Council and Education

Steering Committee; a charter member of the National Association of Negro Business and Professional Women's Club, Inc., and she has served as a board member for the Komen Foundation.

She believes everyone should be afforded the opportunity to grow and fulfill their dreams and their destiny. She has been an advocate for cancer survivors since the early nineties and has supported the work of the Susan G. Komen Foundation in Central East Texas for many years. She serves as a board member for the Good Neighbor Settlement House in Waco, Texas.

Dr. Sandra Henry loves the Lord and is passionate about ministry work. She believes, we are our brother's keepers, and we can build one another up in love. Love humanity enough that through Christ, we give her a lifeline. She also loves gardening, journaling, and spending time with family and friends. She loves welcoming and fellowshipping with dear friends in her home. Dr. Henry loves giving little care bags of hope to those who need uplifting.

*"Life isn't about waiting for the storm to pass;
it's about learning how to dance in the rain."*

~VIVIAN GREEN

*"If you don't like something change it, if you
can't change it, change your attitude."*

~MAYA ANGELOU

*"Now faith is the substance of things hoped for,
the evidence of things not seen"*

~HEBREW 11:1 NKJV

I believe God!

Fear Not, All is Well

~ISAIAH 41:10 NKJV